GEORGE B. POST, ARCHITECT

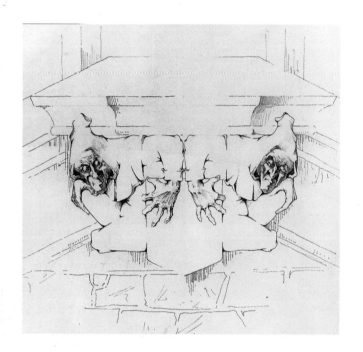

SOURCES OF AMERICAN ARCHITECTURE

GEORGE B. POST, ARCHITECT

PICTURESQUE DESIGNER AND DETERMINED REALIST

———— SARAH BRADFORD LANDAU ————

SERIES EDITOR: ROBERT A. M. STERN

THE MONACELLI PRESS

To my mother

First published in the United States of America in 1998 by
The Monacelli Press, Inc.
10 East 92nd Street, New York, New York 10128.

Library of Congress Cataloging-in-Publication Data
Landau, Sarah Bradford, date.
George B. Post, architect : picturesque designer and
determined realist / Sarah Bradford Landau.
p.   cm.—(Sources of American architecture)
Includes bibliographical references and index.
ISBN 1-885254-92-X
1. Post, George Browne, 1837–1913—Criticism and inter-
pretation. 2. Eclecticism and architecture—United States.
I. Post, George Browne, 1837–1913. II. Title. III. Series.
NA737.P64L36   1998
720'.92—dc21   98-20359

Printed and bound in Singapore

Designed by Abigail Sturges

*Front cover: New York Stock Exchange. Rendering of Broad Street
front by Hughson Hawley (1900), made before the pediment sculpture
program had been determined. Collection of the New-York Historical
Society. (See pl. 20.)*

*Back cover: Williamsburgh Savings Bank. Preliminary rendering
(c.1869). Collection of the New-York Historical Society. (See pl. 2.)*

*Half-title page: Main Building, City College of New York. "Special fig-
ure at High Point, Gable—End of Great Hall." Collection of the New-
York Historical Society. (See fig. 82.)*

Frontispiece: Photograph of George B. Post. From Great American
Architects Series, *no. 4,* Architectural Record *(1898).*

CONTENTS

AUTHOR'S PREFACE
AND ACKNOWLEDGMENTS

George Browne Post's career has intrigued me for many years. My interest was aroused by Winston Weisman's classic study, "The Commercial Architecture of George B. Post," published in the *Journal of the Society of Architectural Historians* in 1972. That stimulating essay included a preliminary list of Post's commissions based on materials in the New-York Historical Society's George B. Post Collection. Seven years later, Leslie Ike's presentation of Post's early work in a seminar offered by Professor Henry-Russell Hitchcock at New York University's Institute of Fine Arts motivated me to examine the Post Collection. By this time I recognized that Post had been greatly underappreciated, not only for his own body of work, but also for his important contributions to the advancement of the profession. This extensive archive, donated to the society by Post's grandson Edward Everett Post, includes Post's job record books, letterbooks, scrapbooks, original drawings and specifications, period photographs, collections of clippings, and records of his successor firm's commissions.

I am indebted to Lisa B. Mausolf, whose 1983 master's thesis for Columbia University, "A Catalog of the Work of George B. Post, Architect," documents more than four hundred of his projects and includes a preliminary listing of his successor firm's projects. Russell Sturgis's "The Works of George B. Post," in *Architectural Record's Great American Architects Series* (1898), was also a fundamental source and provided me with my subtitle, "Picturesque Designer and Determined Realist." Inclusion in the *Great American Architects Series* meant that in his lifetime Post was considered the peer of Adler & Sullivan and McKim, Mead & White.

This book is intended to present Post's most important projects as well as some that are less significant but that reveal his development as a designer and show the range of his firm's production. For the most part, the presentation is chronological, except when there has been a delay in the actual execution of a project or when a comparison helps to illuminate a particular point.

I would like to thank in particular the staff of the New-York Historical Society, especially Mary Beth Betts, Curator of Architecture. Others who have generously helped me and to whom I am indebted are Joyce Rae Inman, Charles J. Quagliana, and Arthur C. Chadek of the Wisconsin State Capitol restoration project; Donald Petit, Cleveland Landmarks Commission; Steven Wheeler, New York Stock Exchange Archivist, and also John R. Kret of the exchange; Marion Kennedy of the Bernardsville Public Library; William J. Dane, Newark Public Library; William O'Malley, formerly of Avery Architectural and Fine Arts Library, Columbia University; Barry Hannegan, Pittsburgh Landmarks Foundation; Marjorie Pearson, New York City Landmarks Preservation Commission; Richard Heaps, Brooklyn Historical Society; Edna Volpe-Way, Hagedorn Gero-Psychiatric Hospital; Sherry Birk, Prints and Drawings Collection, Octagon Museum; Tony Wrenn, American Institute of Architects Library and Archives; Katherine T. Sheehan, Rensselaer County Historical Society; Charles Sachs, formerly of the South Street Seaport Museum; Kenneth R. Cobb, New York City Municipal Archives; and Andrea Monfried of The Monacelli Press.

Among the many who kindly answered my questions, provided photographs, or in other ways assisted me, I am grateful to Mosette Broderick, Douglas G. Bucher, May N. Stone, Jan Hird Pokorny, Isabelle Gournay, Susan Tunick, Sharon Irish, Eric Oxendorf, James T. Potter, Paul F. Miller, Mardges Bacon, Marc Dessauce, Paul David Pearson, Andrew S. Dolkart, Isabelle Hyman, Francis R. Kowsky, Edward Everett Post, and Dorothy S. Post. Lastly, I am especially grateful to my husband, Sidney Landau, for reading the manuscript and making many helpful suggestions.

— S.B.L.

EDITOR'S FOREWORD

George B. Post has been the victim of his own phenomenal success. An exceptional architect, Post has been confined to the historical margins because his most obvious gifts were in the areas of commercial building design and corporate architectural practice. But as Sarah Bradford Landau's insightful overview makes clear, we not only have much to learn from Post's work but can also take pleasure in his accomplishments.

One of the most prolific, prominent, and professional architects in the second half of the nineteenth century, George B. Post combined superb technical skills with a sure and inventive sense of design to advance the science and art of skyscraper design and to address a wide variety of other building types, including luxurious townhouses, banks, college campuses, and state capitols, one of which was built. It was, in fact, the Wisconsin State Capitol with which he crowned his career before leaving his practice to his sons.

Post does not enjoy the wide reputation of his near-contemporary Richard Morris Hunt. Nevertheless, his work exacted the highest respect from his professional peers, including Hunt, and was widely praised by architectural critics. Whereas Hunt, especially in the second half of his career, concentrated on lavish houses for the super-rich, Post consistently pursued the kind of practice that he and Hunt had individually pioneered in the post–Civil War years, addressing virtually any and all kinds of commissions that came along, in terms of both size and character. Although Hunt eventually abandoned the tenements, apartment houses, hotels, and tall buildings of his early years, Post continued true to a conception of architectural practice that can be seen as a prototype, perhaps *the* prototype, of some of the most important and characteristic practices of our own time. In mixing a solid base of commercial work with prestigious residential and especially institutional and government commissions, Post held on to the distinctions inherent in the various building types without losing focus or commitment to overall excellence.

Post was not only talented and well trained, he was also well connected. He was as comfortable with wealthy and influential clients, including Cornelius Vanderbilt II, as he was with colleagues at the office. More importantly, Post was, in his way, equal in managerial skills to the various captains of industry whom he would serve. He was well organized, virtually inventing the modern architectural office, in which a staff was divided into teams, each working on a different project, allowing the architect in charge of the office to work on a number of projects simultaneously.

Though today the collective wisdom tends to emphasize Post's organizational contributions over his achievements as a designer, I believe this is wrong, as Sarah Landau's text so perceptively makes clear. He may not have been an iconoclastic innovator like Louis Sullivan or Frank Lloyd Wright, but he was an innovator nonetheless, notably so in the invention and design of the skyscraper. This book will give readers a long overdue opportunity to reexamine Post's mistakenly overlooked oeuvre and to appreciate anew the work of an architect whose contributions—as designer, engineer, and businessman—were nothing short of seminal.

— R.A.M.S.

COLOR PLATES

*Plate 3. Rendering
(c.1868), possibly
for Presbyterian
Hospital,
New York City.
Collection of
the New-York
Historical Society.*

Plate 4.
Connecticut State
Capitol, Hartford.
Competition
rendering (1871).
Collection of
the New-York
Historical Society.

Plate 5. Dry Dock
Savings Bank,
New York City.
Competition
rendering (1873).
Collection of
the New-York
Historical Society.

Plate 6. Boston
building of the
Mutual Life
Insurance Company
of New York.
Competition
project (c.1873).
Rendering by
E. A. Sargent.
Collection of
the New-York
Historical Society.

Plate 7. Rendering of unidentified residence, probably General Fitz-John Porter House, Morristown, New Jersey (1871–73). Collection of the New-York Historical Society.

*Plate 8. Troy
Savings Bank–
Music Hall,
Troy, New York
(1871–75).
Presentation
rendering (1871).
Collection of
the New-York
Historical Society.*

Plate 9. New York Hospital (1875–77; demolished). Rendering by E. A. Sargent showing hospital as built. Collection of the New-York Historical Society.

Plate 10.
Long Island
(now Brooklyn)
Historical Society,
Brooklyn Heights,
New York
(1878–80).
Photograph
by author.

Plate 11.
Long Island
Historical Society.
Detail of main
entrance.
Photograph
by author.

Plate 14.
Unidentified
church and parish
house. Rendering
(c.1877).
Collection of
the New-York
Historical Society.

Plate 15. C. C.
Baldwin Residence,
Newport, Rhode
Island (addition
1880–81).
Rendering,
front elevation.
Collection of
the New-York
Historical Society.

JAMES H. SEYMOUR & CO.,
COMMISSION MERCHANTS,
159 Chambers Street,
NEW YORK.

BUTTER & EGGS
A SPECIALTY.

COPYRIGHTED BY CALLAHAN & BARLOW.

— THE ★ NEW ★ YORK ★ PRODUCE ★ E

*Plate 16. New York
Produce Exchange
(1881–84;
demolished).
Advertising
poster for
James H. Seymour
& Co., c.1885.
Collection of
the New-York
Historical Society.*

Plate 17.
Apartment house
at 206–208
East 9th Street,
New York City
(1885–86).
Photograph
by author.

Plate 18.
Apartment house
at 206–208
East 9th Street.
Entrance.
The gold paint
is modern.
Photograph
by author.

*Plate 19.
Schermerhorn
Building,
New York City
(1890–91).
Photograph
by author.*

*Plate 20. New York
Stock Exchange
(1901–3).
Rendering of
Broad Street front
by Hughson
Hawley (1900),
made before the
pediment sculpture
program had been
determined.
Collection of
the New-York
Historical Society.*

Plate 22.
Wisconsin State
Capitol, Madison
(1906–17).
Accepted
competition
design (1906).
State of Wisconsin.
Photograph by
Eric Oxendorf.

*Plate 23. Wisconsin
State Capitol. Interior.
Photograph by James T.
Potter, AIA Emeritus.*

GEORGE B. POST, ARCHITECT

THE EARLY YEARS
Commercial Success

If ever a man could be described as destined to succeed, he would be George Browne Post (1837–1913). A New Yorker by birth, he began his career in that city after the Civil War, an opportune place and time for introducing new building types and avant-garde construction technology. Post's assets included more than artistic talent, which he possessed in abundance. He had earned a bachelor's degree in civil engineering and architecture from New York University in 1858, and was then offered the university's professorship in mathematics. Instead, he chose to study architecture in the New York atelier of Richard Morris Hunt.[1] At that time there were no American architecture schools as such; apprentice-training was the usual procedure. Hunt had been trained at the Ecole des Beaux-Arts in Paris, and would not only educate Post but would remain his mentor and loyal supporter over the years. Post also had potential client connections through his family, which was no small advantage. Judging from his later reputation and achievement, he had an extraordinary capacity for managing and coordinating large projects involving many interests and people. In the long run, that strength would perhaps prove to be most important of all his talents.

Post was descended from a prosperous merchant family. His grandfather, Joel Post, had been a successful New York City drug importer, and Post would later name his residence in Bernardsville, New Jersey, Claremont after Joel Post's historic country seat in upper Manhattan.[2] After a military school education at the Churchill School in Ossining, New York, Post became one of the first to study in the new School of Civil Engineering and Architecture at the University of the City of New York, as New York University was then known. As indicated in the university catalog, the

*1. Unidentified
church or chapel.
Gambrill & Post,
architects. Ink
wash rendering
(c.1861–67).
Collection of
the New-York
Historical Society.*

curriculum included "Principles of Architecture, with the elements of Design, Construction, and Estimates," courses in railroad construction and management, a course described as "Science of Masonry and Carpentry, of Machinery, and the Founder's Art," and another in "Linear Drawing, with Color and Shading, as applied to Engineering and Architecture." Post must have especially appreciated the drawing course. He was said to have enjoyed making watercolors and, in later years, to have traveled around Europe indulging that hobby.[3]

Hunt's studio had been in the New York University Building since 1856, and Post must have encountered him there often while he was an engineering student. In 1858, Post, Charles D. Gambrill, and Henry Van Brunt persuaded Hunt to take them on as students, and the following year, Hunt relocated his atelier to larger quarters in his new Tenth Street Studio Building. William Robert Ware and Frank Furness joined the group in 1859. There were other students in the atelier, but these five were the ones who became successful architects, and Ware additionally distinguished himself as an architectural educator. Post later recalled looking to Hunt

> for sympathy and advice with the confident assurance that it would be hearty, true and sound . . . Those of us fortunate enough to be . . . his pupils, will never forget either the wealth of his resources or the inspiring nature of his instruction . . . The study of architecture, at that time, was perused under the most discouraging conditions. The art was ill understood and indeed hardly respected by the public.

Post also alluded to the "literary warfare then prevailing between Gothic and Classic camps" and an "atmosphere, thick with prejudice and controversy."[4]

An important feature of his training with Hunt—one that would serve him in good stead—was learning to draw the classical orders and understand the significance of proportion. The large collection of photographs and books Hunt used in his teaching and made accessible to his students exposed Post to the great architectural monuments of Europe as well as to the avant-garde style of mid-century French architecture known as *Néo-Grec*. Although Hunt was said not to have encouraged his students to work in any particular style, Post was surely well prepared for the Beaux-Arts classicism that flourished in the 1890s and to which he would contribute significantly.[5]

In 1860 Post formed a partnership with Gambrill, which continued until 1867, interrupted only by his service in the Union Army for a period of about eight months during the Civil War. Post became captain of the twenty-second regiment of New York volunteers and also served as a volunteer aide to General Burnside at the battle of Fredericksburg. After the war he eventually attained the rank of colonel of the twenty-second regiment. Nonetheless, his 1887 design for the Twenty-Second Regiment Armory Building was accepted but not executed because it was considered too costly.[6] This was an unusual situation for Post, who was normally very good at keeping costs down.

None of the Gambrill & Post firm's projects can be identified as Post's design, with the possible exception of an ink wash drawing of an unidentified country church where his name appears as delineator (fig. 1). Churches were never to be Post's forte, although he designed at least one that was built (see Chapter 4), and he altered and enlarged several. Among those he altered were the University Place Presbyterian Church (first in 1885 and again in 1895), which his family attended in New York City, and the Basking Ridge, New Jersey, Presbyterian Church (in 1907–8), which was the church he attended when at his country home. Post restored Holy Trinity Church in Brooklyn Heights in 1895.[7] About all that can be said of the early rendering is that Post had a propensity for the picturesque. In 1867 Post started his own New York City practice, remaining independent until 1904 when two of his sons were made partners in the firm of George B. Post & Sons. Meanwhile, Henry Hobson Richardson became Gambrill's new partner in 1867.[8]

Throughout his long career, Post competed for commissions. In fact, his career was made on competitions. Unlike McKim, Mead & White, for example, he welcomed them, although he always insisted that the terms be clear and the conditions fair. His independent practice was launched in 1867 when he entered the competition for the Equitable Life Assurance Society Building (pl. 1). The eight-story project he submitted did not win, but the building committee had difficulty deciding between Post's design and that of the winner, Gilman & Kendall, and the members were evidently impressed by Post's engineering knowledge. He was appointed consulting architect in charge of ironwork, elevators, and vaults, and he also served as supervising architect. After reviewing a bid that he thought was too high, Post redesigned the ironwork and cut the cost of the Equitable Building's extensive internal iron framing by half. The ironwork included inner court walls supported on cast-iron columns; if the engineer and architect William Harvey Birkmire was correct in his assessment, those walls anticipated skeleton construction.[9]

Because it was the first office building to utilize elevators, the Equitable Building (1868–70) is today recognized as having initiated the skyscraper type. Its two steam-powered elevators, designed by Otis Tufts of Boston,

had higher shafts than any built up to that time. Post claimed that it was he who convinced the building committee to allow the building to be six stories or higher—as built, it was eight—and to install elevators. He himself rented the top suite of offices on the Broadway side, remaining until 1879 and apparently resisting a buy-out offer from the owners. Judging from his rendering of the project, Post's building would have been impressive and probably better designed than Gilman & Kendall's (cf. fig. 2). Fashioned in a restrained version of the Second Empire style, it recalls aspects of the New Louvre's Pavillon de la Bibliothèque, on which Hunt had worked in the mid-1850s. The large, arch-topped windows defining the company's two-story-high business hall are a feature Post would continue to develop in future designs. With the Equitable Building, Post's success as a commercial architect was assured, and when the company decided to double the size of the building in the 1880s, he was given the job. Daniel Burnham later called Post the "father of the tall building in New York."[10] That could be said without the qualification of "in New York," for in 1872 Post would design one of the earliest skyscrapers: the Western Union Building in New York.

2. Equitable Life Assurance Society Building, New York City (1868–70; demolished). Gilman & Kendall, architects, and George B. Post. From Robert Blackall, "Photographs of the U.S." Courtesy of the Rotch Visual Collections, MIT.

Post's perspective rendering for a large institutional complex may be a competition drawing for Presbyterian Hospital in New York (pl. 3). If that is so, then in 1868 Post was competing against his former teacher, Hunt, who won the commission. Another possibility, however, is that Post made an alternative rendering for Hunt. Post's practical knowledge of building systems is here represented by a pencil-drawn elevation, affixed to the back of the rendering, describing the ventilation system for the main building and the location of cold-air ducts. Post's central building has a tall spire, indicating the presence of a chapel, as Hunt's main building had. Hunt's hospital as executed fused the *Néo-Grec* with the High Victorian Gothic style then popular for churches and institutional buildings, and linked the pavilions flanking the main building in the French manner. Post's impressive rendering provides a more complete version than Hunt's of the polychromatic High Victorian Gothic; and, although aligned in rows, the flanking buildings appear to be independent. Large institutional buildings, including hospitals, were to be a significant part of Post's production, but rarely did he design in the High Victorian Gothic style.

In 1869–70 Post designed three buildings for the College of New Jersey in Princeton, later renamed Princeton University: the Bonner-Marquand Gymnasium; Dickinson Hall, a classroom building; and a dormitory, Reunion Hall (fig. 3). Unfortunately, not one of them is still standing, an all-too-common fate for Post's buildings. Although pioneering and state-of-the-art for their time, many were replaced by larger buildings in

*3. Princeton College
(College of New Jersey)
in 1875. Lithograph
(numbers added).*

1. Dickinson Hall.
2. Reunion Hall.
*3. Bonner-Marquand
   Gymnasium.*

*Princeton University
Library.*

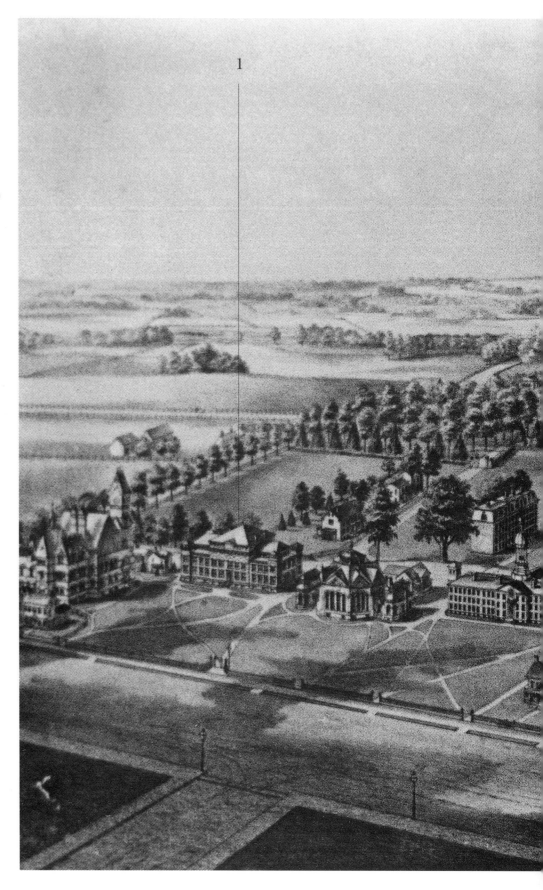

the twentieth century. It is very likely that Post got the Princeton commissions through family connections. John Cleve Green, who financed Dickinson Hall, lived at 10 Washington Square North in New York, not far from Post's family home at 18 Waverly Place. Green was one of New York University's major benefactors while Post was a student there and in the years following. Green's brother, Henry Woodhull Green, was an influential member of Princeton's board of trustees as well as former chancellor of the prerogative court of New Jersey. The gymnasium commission allowed Post to design a large interior space, which he enclosed within a massive, chateaulike exterior with sandstone walls trimmed in brownstone (fig. 4). At the time it was constructed, the gymnasium was said to have been the best building of its kind in the country. It stood until 1907.[11]

However, Post soon lost his footing at Princeton. Another New York architect would be commissioned to design the Chancellor Green Library (1871–73). Constructed in honor of Henry Woodhull Green, the new library was the gift of John Cleve Green. Post had received a questionnaire sent out by Chancellor Green in February of 1871 concerning the best materials, plan, and size for the proposed new library. In March and April, Post wrote letters to Green offering advice on fireproof construction and the plan for the new building. He also requested a personal interview. All of this came to naught. William A. Potter, an architect who had less practical experience than Post but who was also trained in engineering, designed the library in 1871. This beautiful building remains the centerpiece of the campus. Originally built with round arches topping the windows, Post's Dickinson Hall was extensively altered in the mid-1870s by Edward D. Lindsey. Lindsey changed its style to Gothic, doubtless to make the building more compatible with the adjacent Chancellor Green Library and the nearby John C. Green Science Hall (1872–74), another Potter design.[12]

Post's Williamsburgh Savings Bank (1870–75) in Brooklyn fully demonstrates his brilliance as a designer (pl. 2 and figs. 5–7). The building survives and still functions as a bank. Post was invited to compete for the commission along with three other architects, and won. In the opinion of Post's contemporary A. J. Bloor, "outside of governmental and ecclesiastical structures, there is probably no more monumental . . . building in this country than the Williamsburgh Savings Bank." Bloor carefully described its style as "Renaissance tinged with Neo-Grec feeling though motivated by Roman examples."[13] All the lessons learned in Hunt's atelier, and possibly the inspiration of Hunt's Lenox Library in New York, on which construction also began in 1870, came to fruition here. Indeed, the bank's style

was precocious. Although the temple front and domed banking room had been stylish for banks early in the century, the palazzo mode and subsequent Second Empire style had since displaced those forms. The Williamsburgh Savings Bank set precedents not only for Post's future bank buildings but also for the monumental Beaux-Arts bank buildings to come.[14] Comparison of Post's preliminary perspective rendering to the building as constructed reveals that he decided to increase the height of the dome and add a lantern in the Renaissance manner, undoubtedly to make the building more visible in the cityscape and more prestigious in appearance (cf. pl. 2 and fig. 5).

Illuminated from the sides and by a ring of windows surrounding the base of the lofty dome, the large banking hall is enhanced by polished granite and marble facings, finely detailed moldings and pilaster capitals, and bronze grilles with sunflowers over the heat registers. Peter B. Wight was responsible for the decoration of this impressive interior.

4. Bonner-Marquand Gymnasium, Princeton College (1869; demolished). Princeton University Library.

Wight's rather ordinary Second Empire–style design had taken second place in the competition, but Post had expected him to win—probably because Wight's brother-in-law was on the bank's board—and had made a deal with him to the effect that whoever won would employ the other to assist with the project. Wight's handiwork includes the delicate, English-inspired polychromatic decoration in the dome (fig. 7). English tiles added color to the floor.[15] Throughout his career, Post engaged top-notch artists to decorate his interiors, and gave careful attention to every detail. The banking hall's large open space and cast-iron-framed, double-shell dome on pendentives are the result of Post's engineering skill and good sense of proportion.

In 1871 Post participated in an invited competition for the new Connecticut State Capitol (pl. 4). Five architects submitted projects. Post described the style of his submission as

> that which has developed in the erection of . . . many . . . public buildings of France—And is, I think, far more appropriate, and know it to be more economical, than the huge mass of columns, cornices, & pediments usual in such structures—whose great projections cast a dark shade into the windows and whose effect is rather showy, than dignified and elegant.

Post disparaged any scheme where "the mass was dwarfed by its own dome," an interesting statement in light of his later Beaux-Arts Wisconsin State Capitol, where the huge dome dominates the mass but does not overpower it.[16] There is a striking resemblance between his competition entry for the Connecticut Capitol and the Williamsburgh Savings Bank, where pilasters also frame a tall arch above the main entrance, but the capitol design most effectively omits the pediment.

Unable to come to a decision, the Capitol Commission announced a second competition and invited other architects to compete against the original five. The process was badly handled throughout, and the architects were given insufficient time to prepare. In the end, Richard Michell Upjohn's unorthodox High Victorian Gothic submission was selected and executed. This was not the only time Post's radical *Néo-Grec*—that is, radical for its time in America—lost to that Ruskin-influenced style. In 1873 Leopold Eidlitz's High Victorian Gothic design for the Dry Dock Savings Bank in New York was selected over Post's entry (pl. 5).

Post and Wight collaborated on another project in 1871, a house for General Fitz-John Porter in Morristown, New Jersey (pl. 7). Although never a major focus in Post's practice, residential commissions were undertaken with some regularity throughout his career. In this instance, Wight, having decided to move to Chicago after accepting the commission, turned the

6. Williamsburgh
Savings Bank.
First-floor interior
looking east.
Photograph by
Carl Forster.
New York City
Landmarks
Preservation
Commission.

7. Williamsburgh
Savings Bank.
Dome interior.
Photograph by
Carl Forster.
New York City
Landmarks
Preservation
Commission.

project over to Post.[17] Here again, Post is indebted to Hunt. The gabled and towered house with its large veranda resembles his teacher's picturesque Newport, Rhode Island, "cottages" of the 1860s and early 1870s.

The Troy Savings Bank–Music Hall (1871–75) in Troy, New York, is another early Post masterpiece, and called for an unusual combination of uses that he must have found challenging (pl. 8 and fig. 8). It is possible that Post won this commission because he alone among the invited competitors met the building committee's estimated-costs requirement. His competence in iron construction was very likely also a factor, something that can be appreciated in the roof construction, where curved, rolled-iron trusses support the slate roof and penthouse, and iron bars extending from the trusses carry an iron grid to which the Music Hall's coved plaster ceiling is attached (fig. 9). The ventilation ducts were housed inside the roof.

8. Troy Savings Bank–Music Hall, Troy, New York (1871–75). From stereopticon photograph of 1875 by Leo Daft. Collection of the Rensselaer County Historical Society, Troy, New York.

Large open interiors for public use, unobstructed by vertical supports, were by now Post's specialty. The Troy Music Hall gave him the opportunity to design a 60-foot-high space, 110 feet deep by 75 feet wide and capable of seating 1,250 people (fig. 10). The original first-floor lobby and banking hall were also impressive spaces (fig. 11). Although alterations have been made to the building, including lighting and minor structural changes by Post's successor firm in 1929, the Music Hall itself is largely intact.[18]

With its paired columns framing big windows, subtle polychromy achieved through the use of contrasting materials, curved roof, and circle motifs, the exterior of the Troy Savings Bank–Music Hall may be indebted to the Paris Opera, but it also recalls the more restrained Théâtre du Châtelet (1859–62) in Paris by Gabriel Davioud, a *Néo-Grec* practitioner. Even in the unlikely event that Post had not yet traveled in Europe, he knew about developments in French architecture and had access to professional journals from abroad thanks to his training with Hunt. Hunt would certainly have encouraged his students to travel, and it was customary for aspiring architects to tour the major European cities.

Another competition brought Post the opportunity to design the first ten-story office building. This was the Western Union Building (1872–75) in New York (fig. 12). Post bested Hunt and Arthur Gilman, who with his partner Edward Kendall had designed the Equitable Building, among other invited competitors. Bloor described the finished building as "a bold and towering performance in Renaissance of the modern type, which he [Post] has done so much to extend, and of the

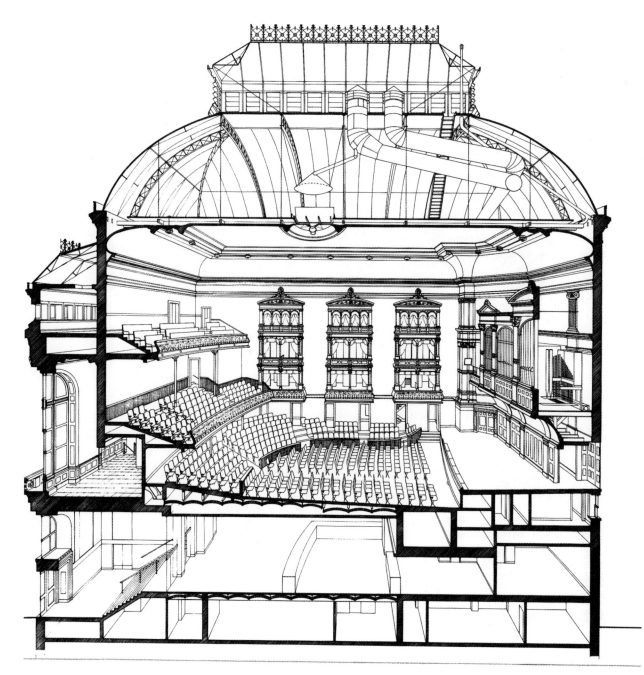

*9. Troy Savings
Bank–Music Hall.
Longitudinal
section looking
north as of 1983.
Drawing by
Douglas G. Bucher
of John Waite
Associates,
Architects.*

*10. Troy Savings
Bank–Music Hall.
Music Hall interior.
From H. R. Page
& Co.,* Troy
Illustrated *(1891).
Collection of the
Rensselaer County
Historical Society,
Troy, New York.*

*11. Troy Savings
Bank–Music Hall.
Bank interior
looking southwest,
in 1940.
Collection of the
Rensselaer County
Historical Society,
Troy, New York.*

sub-type partially suggestive of an engineering standpoint, which has become peculiar to him." But Bloor criticized the superstructure, particularly the roof, which he thought was "rendered picturesque at the cost of repose" and "not without a suspicion of coarseness." He regretted that the "quieter-toned stone selected by the architect for the banding should have been replaced, for economical reasons, by that which has been used."[19] In fact, the organization of the street elevations was more or less tripartite, and the design emphasized the piers, hence, the structural system. Post's gridlike wall treatment represented an American style that might be called the "commercial Neo-Grec," as practiced by Hunt and others as well.

The real triumphs of the Western Union Building were its plan and technology. Many of the functional aspects were of necessity dictated by the telegraph wires essential to the company's operations. Even the iron-railed balcony above the seventh floor served a practical purpose: initially, the telegraph wires entered the building at this point. The iron-framed mansard roof that Bloor so disliked housed lunchroom facilities for the workers on the ninth floor and bedrooms for the engineer and steward on the tenth, as well as space for storage and mechanical equipment. The entire twenty-three-foot-high eighth floor, where the telegraph operators worked, was unobstructed by walls or columns except for the four iron pillars supporting the iron clock tower. Post designed it with tall windows that allowed for maximum natural lighting. In case the water supply in lower Manhattan should prove inadequate in the event of a fire, the building was equipped with its own emergency water-pumping system, and one of its three elevators was an early hydraulic-gravity passenger elevator.[20]

While the Western Union Building was under construction, Post competed unsuccessfully for the Boston headquarters of the Mutual Life Insurance Company of New York. His corner-oriented, Second Empire–style design would have had nine stories including the attic (pl. 6). However, the Boston firm of Peabody & Stearns won this limited competition, and its project for a seven-story building—also Second Empire, but featuring a two-hundred-foot-high clock tower with an observation gallery—was completed in 1875.[21] Perhaps Post was hoping that Mutual Life would follow Western Union's lead and build taller.

Chickering Hall (1874–75) in New York again combined a commercial enterprise, that of selling pianos, with a concert hall (fig. 13). One of Post's finest designs, the building was constructed on the corner of Fifth Avenue and West 18th Street in the entertainment district around Union

12. Western Union Building, New York City (1872–75; demolished). Collection of the New-York Historical Society.

*13. Chickering
Hall, New York
City (1874–75;
demolished).
Collection of
the New-York
Historical Society.*

Square. The Chickering company's pianos were displayed on the first floor, and the concert hall, where "high-class musical entertainment" was offered, was on the second floor. Rhythmically articulated by broad, segmental-arched windows at the first-story level, round-arched two-story arcades at the auditorium level, and a band of small, square-headed windows below the eaves, the exterior again recalls Hunt's Lenox Library. Post used tiles in the spandrels between the round arches to add color to the brick walls, and decorative metal railings designed in the Aesthetic Movement manner with a repeated flower motif also enriched the exterior. Frederick C. Merry, who was Post's assistant at the time, was involved in this project, as he would be in the firm's New York Hospital commission. By this time there were nine people working in Post's office.[22]

Post's engineering and planning skills undoubtedly helped him win the competition for New York Hospital's new building in 1874 (pl. 9). The fact that his great-uncle, the eminent Dr. Wright Post, had been the hospital's attending surgeon may also have predisposed the building committee in his favor. Because of the limitations of the site on West 15th Street between Fifth and Sixth avenues, the new hospital was not designed according to the pavilion plan then favored for hospitals. Instead, it was built as a seven-story block, with a taller central portion and rear wing, and of course, there were elevators. At the time, this deviation from the pavilion scheme was widely criticized, but in the twentieth century, the vertical plan became the standard, and Post's building is credited with setting a precedent for future hospitals. A skylighted solarium on the top floor, used as a recreation hall, was one of the building's special features.[23] In spite of its ornamental metalwork, banded arches, and colorful tile insets, the pressed brick facade was on the whole rather restrained. The arches suggest that Post was already reacting to H. H. Richardson's work. Bloor, who did offer some minor criticisms, considered the street facade "a piece of art-work" and "one of the most striking fronts in the city."[24] In his description of the finished building, written for the building committee, Post frankly states that his goal was utility, not beauty:

> the first consideration . . . should be to secure the most perfect arrangements to administer to the needs of the patients, to give them every possible advantage of comfort, light and ventilation, and thus to secure to them the best chance for ultimate recovery . . . I should therefore be most culpable if I sacrificed any utilitarian considerations, even most remotely affecting this end, to aesthetical considerations of proportion or architectural effect.[25]

He was proud of the building's fireproof construction and its fan-driven ventilation and steam-heating system, which was quite advanced for the time (fig. 14). And he was careful to point out that his original cost estimate had proved to be reliable. This commission also involved altering an

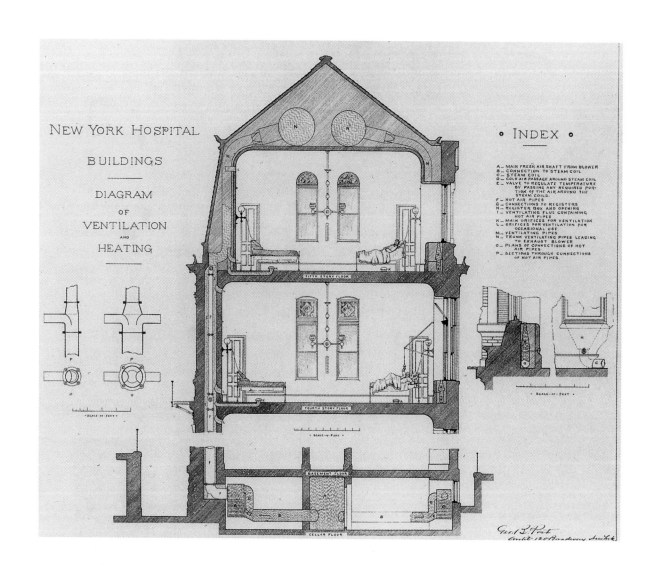

34

14. New York Hospital (1875–77; demolished). Diagram of ventilation and heating. Collection of the New-York Historical Society.

15. Henry M. Braem House, New York City (1878–80; demolished). From Architectural Record *2 (1892).*

existing house, the Thorn mansion on West 16th Street, to serve as the administration building, and in 1890–91, he would add a nurses' residence to the hospital complex.

Another of Post's accomplishments in the 1870s was his use of terra cotta rather than stone trimming. The elaborately ornamented townhouse (1878–80) he designed for the iron merchant and consul Henry M. Braem was one of the earliest New York buildings to feature terra cotta (fig. 15). It was credited as having been "the first strictly architectural terra cotta building" in New York, and the ornament embellishing its brick facade was sculpted with wood-carving tools when the clay was partly dry rather than being modeled in the customary way.[26] Isaac Scott, a craftsman and designer who worked for the Chicago Terra Cotta Company, and who invented this method, did the work. Post's choice of red terra cotta to match the brick of the facade was also innovative, given that a grayish, stonelike color was the usual preference for terra-cotta ornament.[27]

In many respects the exterior of Post's Long Island Historical Society building (1878–80) resembles Chickering Hall. It is one of his masterworks and, fortunately, is still standing (pl. 10). Post won the limited competition, besting Alexander Jackson Davis and Richard Michell Upjohn, among others. The specifications called for a large lecture room on the ground floor; a twenty-five-foot-high library with alcoves at the sides on the second floor, to be reached from the main entrance; and a museum, meeting room, and librarian's office on the floor above the library. Before construction began, Post presented three proposals to the building committee. Two perspective renderings in the Post Collection, one labeled "rejected drawing" and the other, close to the final design, were probably among the drawings he showed the committee[28] (pls. 12 and 13). As completed, the building included all of the items specified. There are four floors, the third incorporating the library gallery and two parlors, one for ladies, the other for gentlemen.

Along with the Braem house, the Long Island Historical Society building was one of the earliest in the New York area to use terra-cotta trim. Originally it was to have been trimmed in brownstone, but during construction, Post decided to substitute terra cotta because of the difficulty involved in getting the brownstone, and because terra cotta was less expensive and could be more easily worked.[29] In a group of "Inspirational Designs" that belonged to Post's firm, there is a view of the Palais de l'Industrie built for the Paris Exposition of 1855 (fig. 16). That structure's arcading and ceramic spandrel decoration may have influenced

*16. Palais de
l'Industrie, Paris
Exposition of 1855
(demolished).
J.-M.-V. Viel,
architect. Collection
of the New-York
Historical Society.*

17. *"Plan for
a Colony of
Tenements."*
From Plumber
and Sanitary
Engineer 2 *(1879).*

Post here. In fact, Post had produced a design in 1869 for an art institute proposed for New York City that was almost a copy of the French exhibition pavilion.[30] The society building's warm red brick walls are matched in color by red terra-cotta sculptural ornament. The ornament includes native American plants in the archivolts, portrait heads of famous men in medallions, and the symbolic heads of a Norseman and an Indian in the spandrels of the main entrance (pl. 11). The sculptor Olin Levi Warner was responsible for the heads. The terra-cotta ornament, the basket-weave brick pattern in the spandrels of the first floor arches, the ironwork railing, and the decoration throughout the building—even the brass doorknobs—were designed in accord with Aesthetic Movement taste.

The structural system was advanced for the time. Cast-iron columns in the lecture hall support the library floor, and the library ceiling is suspended from two iron trusses in the attic, which also support the roof and attic floor. Ceilings were commonly suspended from trusses, but Post may have been one of the first architects to suspend a floor from a truss system in the manner of bridge construction. The library galleries are supported by slim cast-iron columns enclosed within carved wood columns. The ventilating system, which involved air shafts and concealed ducts, was also innovative.[31]

Among Post's designs, there is one for an unidentified, undated church and parish house (pl. 14) that is clearly influenced by H. H. Richardson, especially his Trinity Church in Boston. The round, bichromatic arches, heavy crossing tower, and checkered pattern in the gables are all Richardsonian. The probable date of Post's rendering is 1877, the year Trinity Church was completed and published in *American Architect and Building News.*[32] Although Post would not fully embrace the Richardsonian Romanesque until the mid-1880s, this rendering and his design for New York Hospital suggest his early appreciation of Richardson's work.

In 1879, in collaboration with the civil engineer George W. Dresser, Post produced a plan for a group of tenement houses organized within a system of auxiliary east-west streets (fig. 17). Along with Edward T. Potter and other architects, Post was dissatisfied with the limitations of the city's grid plan and became interested in tenement reform, likely because he himself had designed tenements and expected to produce more of them. His design efforts and his recognized professional status by the 1890s led to his appointment to the New York Tenement House Commission in 1894.[33] At the other end of the residential spectrum, Post received a commission in 1879 that would result in the grandest house of his career, Cornelius Vanderbilt's New York City mansion. This was an auspicious beginning for the 1880s.

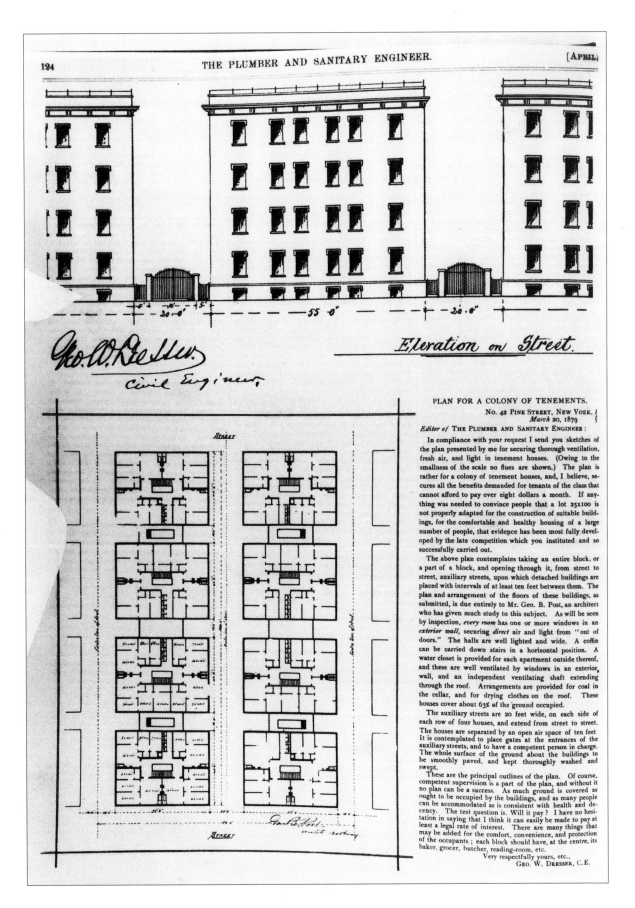

Elevation on Street.

Geo. W. Dresser,
Civil Engineer.

PLAN FOR A COLONY OF TENEMENTS.

No. 42 PINE STREET, NEW YORK, }
March 20, 1879 {

Editor of THE PLUMBER AND SANITARY ENGINEER :

In compliance with your request I send you sketches of the plan presented by me for securing thorough ventilation, fresh air, and light in tenement houses. (Owing to the smallness of the scale no flues are shown.) The plan is rather for a colony of tenement houses, and, I believe, secures all the benefits demanded for tenants of the class that cannot afford to pay over eight dollars a month. If anything was needed to convince people that a lot 25x100 is not properly adapted for the construction of suitable buildings, for the comfortable and healthy housing of a large number of people, that evidence has been most fully developed by the late competition which you instituted and so successfully carried out.

The above plan contemplates taking an entire block, or a part of a block, and opening through it, from street to street, auxiliary streets, upon which detached buildings are placed with intervals of at least ten feet between them. The plan and arrangement of the floors of these buildings, as submitted, is due entirely to Mr. Geo. B. Post, an architect who has given much study to this subject. As will be seen by inspection, *every room* has one or more windows in an *exterior wall*, securing *direct* air and light from "out of doors." The halls are well lighted and wide. A coffin can be carried down stairs in a horizontal position. A water closet is provided for each apartment outside thereof, and these are well ventilated by windows in an exterior wall, and an independent ventilating shaft extending through the roof. Arrangements are provided for coal in the cellar, and for drying clothes on the roof. These houses cover about 63% of the ground occupied.

The auxiliary streets are 20 feet wide, on each side of each row of four houses, and extend from street to street. The houses are separated by an open air space of ten feet It is contemplated to place gates at the entrances of the auxiliary streets, and to have a competent person in charge. The whole surface of the ground about the buildings to be smoothly paved, and kept thoroughly washed and swept.

These are the principal outlines of the plan. Of course, competent supervision is a part of the plan, and without it no plan can be a success. As much ground is covered as ought to be occupied by the buildings, and as many people can be accommodated as is consistent with health and decency. The test question is. Will it pay? I have no hesitation in saying that I think it can easily be made to pay at least a legal rate of interest. There are many things that may be added for the comfort, convenience, and protection of the occupants ; each block should have, at the centre, its baker, grocer, butcher, reading-room, etc.

Very respectfully yours, etc.,
GEO. W. DRESSER, C.E.

CHAPTER 2

THE 1880s

Mansions, the New York Produce Exchange, Skyscrapers, and More

Why Cornelius Vanderbilt selected Post, and not Richard Morris Hunt, as architect for his Fifth Avenue mansion is open to speculation. Certainly there were direct connections between Post and the Vanderbilts. Mrs. Cornelius Vanderbilt's brother, David E. Gwynne, had served with Post in the twenty-second regiment during the Civil War, and Cornelius Vanderbilt was already a major stockholder in the Western Union Telegraph Company and a member of the building committee when Post won that commission. Post and Vanderbilt were fellow members of the Century Association.[1] On the other hand, Hunt was already working for Cornelius's brother, William K. Vanderbilt. Hunt had designed the latter's Long Island country house, and at the same time that Post's Cornelius Vanderbilt mansion (1879–82) was under construction, Hunt's city mansion for William K. Vanderbilt was rising nearby. Both mansions were part of what has often been called "Vanderbilt Row" on the west side of Fifth Avenue: Cornelius's at the corner of West 57th Street and his brother's at West 52nd Street just to the north of the contemporary twin mansions of their father, W. H. Vanderbilt, and their sisters between West 51st and 52nd streets. The Vanderbilts had recently inherited considerable sums of money from W. H. Vanderbilt's father, railroad magnate Commodore Vanderbilt, and their grand mansions were conspicuous expressions of those legacies.[2]

The sons' residences were styled to resemble French chateaus, Hunt's in gray limestone with intricate Gothic details, and Post's in brick, trimmed with light stone, and more Renaissance in style (fig. 18). There seems to be no question that Hunt invented their *François I* style. In fact, Post had probably seen Hunt's unexecuted design of 1870 for the Jim Fisk house, because the Cornelius Vanderbilt mansion was similarly handled with

18. Cornelius Vanderbilt Mansion, New York City (1879–82). Collection of the New-York Historical Society.

prominent stone banding and small corner turrets, and the Fisk house was also intended to be brick trimmed with stone.[3] Once again, Post was Hunt's pupil.

Cornelius Vanderbilt soon became dissatisfied with his mansion. A few years after it was finished, he consulted Ernest Flagg, his cousin by marriage, who drew plans for altering and enlarging the mansion. Flagg recalled that Vanderbilt was "very much dissatisfied with the plan of his house . . . what he really wanted was more and larger rooms."[4] Vanderbilt later asked Hunt to design an addition, but Hunt refused, saying that the architect who had built the house should do the alterations. He did, however, recommend that a tower be included to relieve the "monotony of the Fifth Avenue facade." Hunt did not charge Vanderbilt for this advice, and in a note to him explained that "it was only an act of comradeship for my old friend Post."[5] In the end, Post got the commission, but Hunt was chosen to design Vanderbilt's Newport, Rhode Island, mansion known as the Breakers (1892–95).

Post's enlargement of the Fifth Avenue mansion (1892–94) expanded it northward and westward (figs. 19–21). It included a towerlike addition, as recommended by Hunt, at the north end of the Fifth Avenue front and a formidable porte cochere with reliefs by Karl Bitter at the new main entrance on West 58th Street. In its expanded form, the mansion was ostentatiously huge and included grander and more elaborately decorated interiors than the original structure (fig. 22). Russell Sturgis was polite about the changes:

> The original house . . . was a concentrated, energetic expression of an idea, and was as good a piece of French Renaissance modified to meet New York requirements as we are likely to see . . . but the larger house lacks that unity of design.[6]

Instead, Sturgis preferred to discuss the artistic interiors. The original decorative work by John La Farge, Augustus Saint-Gaudens, and other Aesthetic Movement artists remained, but much of it was relocated in the process of expansion. Post's incredibly detailed section drawings showing the exotic interiors with guests in the major rooms and servants moving about the house must have impressed the Vanderbilts (fig. 23). These were exhibited at the Architectural League in 1894. When the mansion was partly dismantled prior to its demolition in 1927, some elements were saved, including one pair of the two monumental iron entrance gates and two of Karl Bitter's porte-cochere reliefs. The reliefs are just inside the entrance of the nearby Sherry Netherland Hotel, constructed in 1927, and since 1939, the gates have been at the Fifth Avenue entrance of the Central Park Conservatory Garden.[7]

*19. Cornelius
Vanderbilt Mansion.
Charcoal rendering
by J. Vincent
(c.1892) showing
West 58th Street
front of house as it
was to be enlarged.
Collection of
the New-York
Historical Society.*

44

*20. Cornelius
Vanderbilt Mansion
(1879–82; 1892–94;
demolished). The
house at the right
(1880–82; demol-
ished), built for
W. J. Hutchinson,
was also designed by
Post. From* New York
Architect *3 (1909).*

*21. Cornelius
Vanderbilt
Mansion
as enlarged.
West 57th Street
front. Collection of
the New-York
Historical Society.*

22. Cornelius Vanderbilt Mansion. Grand salon. Decorated by Jules Allard et ses Fils. Collection of the New-York Historical Society.

*23. Cornelius
Vanderbilt
Mansion.
Longitudinal
section looking
west through
center suite of
rooms (c.1892).
Collection of
the New-York
Historical Society.*

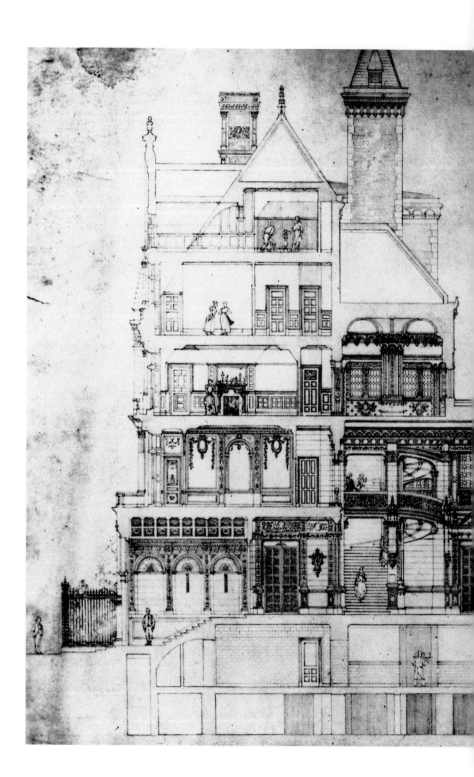

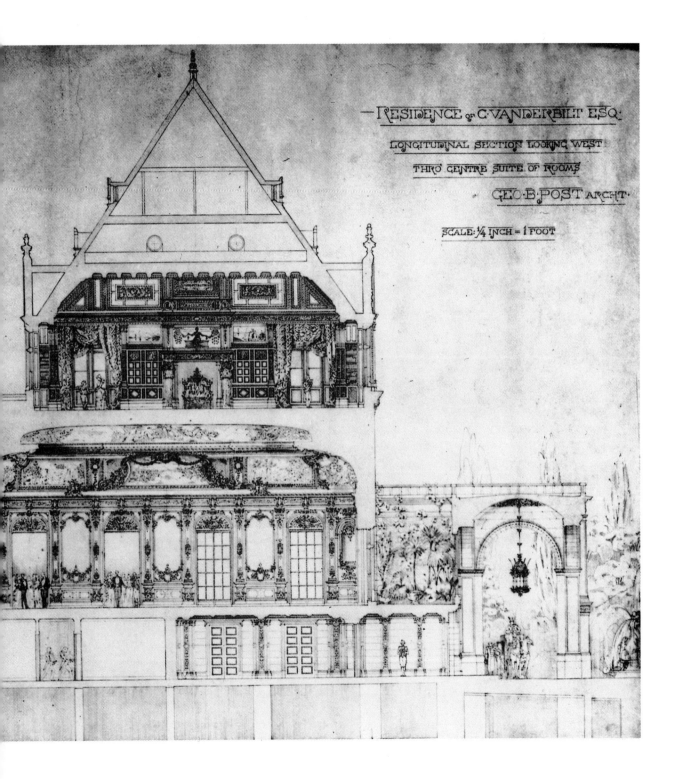

—RESIDENCE of C. VANDERBILT ESQ.

LONGITUDINAL SECTION LOOKING WEST

THRO' CENTRE SUITE OF ROOMS

GEO. B. POST ARCHT.

SCALE: ¼ INCH = 1 FOOT

*24. Post Building,
New York City
(1880–82; demol-
ished). Presentation
drawing. Collection
of the New-York
Historical Society.*

In 1880 Post designed an addition for the C. C. Baldwin house in Newport, Rhode Island (pl. 15). The addition, which transformed the appearance of the house, is styled in the Old English manner of Richard Norman Shaw's houses in England. Richardson's William Watts Sherman house (1874–75), also in Newport, is recognized as the first American expression of that style, and Post had quickly followed suit. He based the Baldwin house on his own unbuilt project of about 1877 for the Newport house of James Gordon Bennett, owner of the *New York Herald.* Known as Chateau-Nooga, to commemorate Baldwin's promotion in 1880 to president of the Louisville & Nashville Railroad Company, Post's red and yellow brick house with its big woody gables, faux half-timbering, and shingled upper walls is fortunately still standing.[8]

Office buildings make up Post's most important work of the 1880s. His projects incorporated innovations in plan, construction technology, and style. His father and uncle, Joel Browne Post and John Alexander Post respectively, were his clients for the Post Building (1880–82), which initiated the U-shaped office block (fig. 24). This eight-and-a-half-story building was at the juncture of Exchange Place, Beaver Street, and Hanover Street in lower Manhattan. Because of the way it was formed, with wings above the base, the inner offices received more light and air than the typical interior court would have allowed. Other distinguishing features were the tripartite facade organization, a development in New York commercial work of the 1870s and 1880s that is especially notable in Post's designs; the arcaded facade treatment; the rounded corners; and the remarkably open, two-story base. The Post Building was also unusual for its time in being uniformly light in color above its bluestone base. Its pale yellow brick exterior was trimmed in matching terra cotta. Schuyler praised the Post Building, calling its style "free Renaissance," and Sturgis admired its "straight-forward and simple design" and considered it "altogether one of the best business buildings we have."[9] The U-shaped plan would be used well into the twentieth century for commercial buildings, apartment houses, and hotels covering large areas.

Post's Mills Building (1881–83) was a much larger nine-and-a-half-story office block constructed on Broad Street at the corner of Exchange Place (figs. 25 and 26). It was also U-shaped above the base, but its commercial Neo-Grec style, materials, and color scheme were more like those of the Western Union Building. A flat roof and narrow, bearing-wall piers framing large windows gave the building a precociously modern appearance. The client, millionaire philanthropist Darius Ogden Mills, spared no expense. This was the first office building in New York—perhaps the first in the world—to have its own electricity-generating plant. The Mills

*25. Mills Building,
New York City
(1881–83; demol-
ished). Collection
of the New-York
Historical Society.*

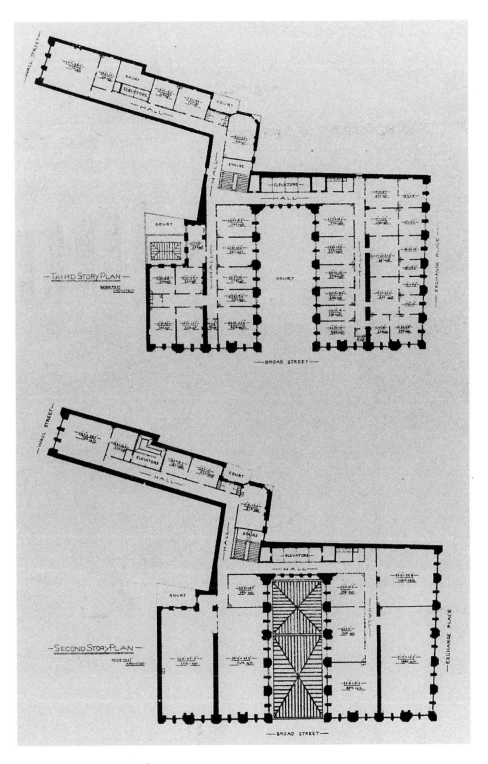

26. Mills Building.
Second- (bottom)
and third-story plans.
From Builder *44*
(1883).

27. Mills Building.
Iron grille at
entrance. Collection
of the New-York
Historical Society.

*28. New York
Produce Exchange
(1881–84; demol-
ished). Collection
of the New-York
Historical Society.*

Building was also equipped with six hydraulic elevators and a restaurant on the top floor that was large enough to serve all the tenants of its three hundred offices. A magnificent wrought-iron grille at the main entrance could be lowered by hydraulic power to close off the skylighted lobby (fig. 27). The handsome Aesthetic Movement design was calculated so that when the grille was in the raised position, its arch met the stone arch over the entrance.[10] No sooner was the building finished than Post was called upon to enlarge it along Exchange Place.

Without question, Post's New York Produce Exchange (1881–84), sited at 2 Broadway opposite Bowling Green, was his commercial masterpiece and one of the great buildings of the Victorian era (pl. 16 and fig. 28). In 1880 Post was invited to compete for this important commission. The specifications called for a large, skylighted exchange room with a spacious interior light court above it. Given his experience designing large interior spaces, Post was well-suited to take on this challenge. His Renaissance arcading emphasizing "the value of repeated openings" impressed the building committee.[11]

As constructed, the exterior featured a four-story-high arcade defining a huge, sixty-four-foot-high exchange room inside (fig. 29). A two-story arcade representing two office floors over the aisles of the exchange room doubled the rhythm, and the composition was terminated by a band of rectangular openings that again doubled the rhythm and a cornicelike, arcaded attic story. This extraordinary rhythmic treatment would influence both Richardson's Marshall Field Wholesale Store (1885–87) and Adler & Sullivan's Auditorium Building (1887–90) in Chicago. Visible from miles away, the Produce Exchange's campanilelike clock tower contained elevators and a staircase. Post described his style as "modified Italian Renaissance, with strongly developed horizontal cornices."[12] Likely sources of inspiration included Henri Labrouste's Bibliothèque Sainte Geneviève and towered European town halls, especially the Berlin Rathaus (1859–70) by H. F. Waesemann.

The exchange building's red brick and matching red-terra-cotta-trimmed walls were relieved only by the light-toned granite at the base and framing the entrances. The symbolic relief ornament in the spandrels of the arches and between the sixth and seventh floors was executed by sculptors Edward Kemeys and Domingo Mora using red terra cotta supplied by the Perth Amboy Terra Cotta Company. Animal heads and also state seals in the roundels were prominent features. As usual, Post made sure he secured the best talent available.[13]

*29. New York
Produce Exchange.
Interior of exchange
room. From* King's
Handbook of
New York City
(1893 edition).

New York Produce Exchange.

SET 2
H

TRANSVERSE SECTION ON LINE C–D

SCALE 4 FOUR FEET TO THE INCH
THIS DRAWING TO BE RETURNED TO
Geo. B. Post. Architect.
COURTLAND ST. N.Y. CITY

30. *New York
Produce Exchange.
Transverse section
drawing. Collection
of the New-York
Historical Society.*

31. *New York
Produce Exchange.
View of exchange
room under
construction.
Collection of
the New-York
Historical Society.*

The Produce Exchange's interior iron framing was at the cutting edge technologically (figs. 30 and 31). The most important innovation was Post's early use of skeleton, or skyscraper, construction for the inner court walls. Bearing walls, like the outer walls of the exchange, would become obsolete for tall buildings within the next decade. Once again, Post was a pioneer. With the demolition of this building in 1957, the nation lost a truly magnificent work.

32. New York Cotton Exchange (1883–85; demolished). Collection of the New-York Historical Society.

Yet another invited competition brought Post the New York Cotton Exchange commission (1883–85). Responding to the oddly shaped site at Hanover Square and William and Beaver streets, Post designed an asymmetrical nine-story building with a shallow, U-shaped light court and rounded entrance front topped by a high, conical roof (fig. 32). Set off by the red slate roof, the exterior walls were again uniformly light, and the suspended ceiling construction of the exchange room was of the same type as that used for the Troy Music Hall.[14]

Post's Mortimer Building (1884–85), constructed at the corner of Wall and New streets, was not well received by the press (fig. 33). For example: "Six storys of little arched openings, all virtually of the same size, all grouped alike, all shaped alike and all treated alike do not exactly suggest an exuberant and ever-changing fancy."[15] Winston Weisman criticized both the Cotton Exchange and the Mortimer Building as awkward solutions to problem sites, but again Post was probably putting function first.[16] His New York Stock Exchange would later adjoin the Mortimer Building.

While these office buildings were rising, Post was also producing housing. As early as 1872 he had designed a structure described in New York building department records as "French flats" for William Black; it had commercial space on the ground floor and a lodge room on the top floor.[17] *French flats* was the term then used to describe the small apartment house. Although much altered, the seven-story Black Building (1872–74) still stands on the northeast corner of Fifth Avenue and East 28th Street. Charles E. Rhinelander financed four French flats buildings (1883–84) near the southwest corner of Third Avenue and East 89th Street. Two years later, again working for Rhinelander, Post planned eight tenements that filled the block on the west side of First Avenue between East 89th and 90th streets (1886–87); the four that remain at 1729–1735 First Avenue have been greatly altered. Rhinelander, a major real estate developer in the city, was related to the Posts, which may explain these commissions. For James Thomson, Post built an eleven-family apartment house (1885–86) at 206–208 East 9th Street near Third Avenue (pls. 17 and 18).

The Mortimer Building
New York : (City)
Mr. George B Post : Architect:

Here, the exuberant terra-cotta ornament, entrance doors, and even the foyer floor tiles are intact.

The survival rate of Post's low-rise commercial buildings in New York is far better than that of his tall office buildings, mainly because many of the smaller structures are in manufacturing districts protected by twentieth-century zoning ordinances. However, Post's loft building at 142–144 Beekman Street (1885) may have survived on the merits of its ornament (figs. 34 and 35). The terra-cotta-trimmed brick facades display fish in the keystones, a cockleshell cornice, and tie-rod washers shaped like starfish. Financed by Ellen S. Auchmuty, a descendant of the prominent Schermerhorn family, this building was occupied until recent years by businesses associated with the Fulton Fish Market.[18]

33. Mortimer Building, New York City (1884–85; demolished). From American Architect and Building News 19 (1886).

As the Equitable Life Assurance Society prospered, its building expanded accordingly. Post was the architect for at least eight alterations over the years, but the major expansion came between 1886 and 1889, when he enlarged the building to fill its blockfront, extended it to Nassau Street, and added two stories under a new mansard roof (figs. 36 and 37). Oddly, Post seems not to have been the first choice for the job. Hunt was offered it, but declined, and Hunt's associate, Edward E. Raht, was also seriously considered.[19] Solving various structural problems in the process, Post created an impressive building styled to match the original structure and having a spectacular new lobby. The lobby became a vaulted corridor leading to an arcade covered by a stained-glass skylighted barrel vault and featuring a mosaic by the Herter Brothers (fig. 38). At either side of the arcade were booths where one could purchase such essentials as telegraph service, train tickets, and umbrellas. The arcade was described as a "novelty in this country" and as being larger and more imposing than "most of the similar structures of Europe."[20] Post was inspired by the arcades of Paris and the Galleria Vittorio Emmanuele in Milan. The walls enclosing the court above the vault were iron-framed in the manner of the court walls of the Produce Exchange.

The New York Times Building (1888–89), Post's next skyscraper, and his only surviving one in lower Manhattan (fig. 39), began as a reconstruction of the old five-story Times Building at the foot of City Hall Park. At thirteen stories, the finished product was effectively a new building, but the lower five floors utilized the old building's floor framing, and in places, the strong new foundations were consolidated with the old ones. During the first phase of construction, the work of producing the newspaper went on while the walls of the new building were rising, a feat that only Post could have managed. The result was cleverly described as "the old Times

34. *142–144*
Beekman Street,
South Street
Seaport,
New York City
(1885).
Photograph by
author.

35. *142–144*
Beekman Street.
Detail of Beekman
Street facade.
Photograph by
author.

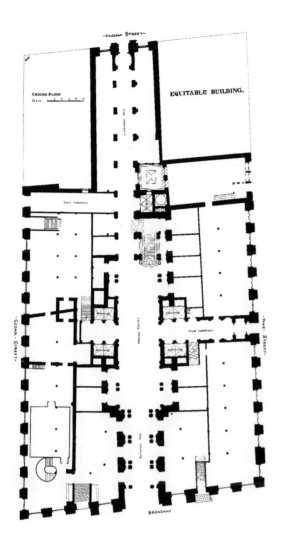

36 (opposite).
Equitable Building
as enlarged,
New York City
(1886–89;
demolished).
The Equitable Life
Assurance Society
of the United States
Archives.

37. Equitable
Building as
enlarged.
Ground-floor plan.
From William
Alexander,
Description
of the New
Equitable
Building . . .
(1887).

building with a new stone overcoat on, a mansard roof for a high hat and a practically new interior."[21] The interior framing was constructed entirely of wrought iron to the eleventh floor. Above that, the interior columns were cast iron, and the outer masonry walls were bearing.

Because of the unusual way the building was constructed, it was logical for Post to treat the first five floors as the base of his complex tripartite composition. Thick iron-reinforced masonry piers inserted at the partition wall determined the four-part vertical division of the long Nassau Street and Park Row facades. Obviously, Richardson's Romanesque style influenced Post here, although the arcaded treatment recalls Post's own Produce Exchange. Post had lost the competition for the Cincinnati Chamber of Commerce to Richardson, and was undoubtedly familiar with that building. After the Times moved to its West 42nd Street building, Robert Maynicke, who had been a member of Post's staff, altered and enlarged Post's building for its new owner. While he was in Post's office, Maynicke had supervised the construction of the Troy Savings Bank–Music Hall, the Mills Building, and the enlargement of the Equitable Building, and he

*38. Equitable
Building as
enlarged. Arcade.
The Equitable Life
Assurance Society
of the United States
Archives.*

would do the same for three more of the firm's New York office buildings: the World, Union Trust, and Havemeyer buildings.[22]

Montgomery Schuyler considered Post's Union Trust Building (1889–90) to be the first to enforce "powerfully" the tripartite composition of base, shaft, and capital[23] (fig. 40). Although Post never restricted himself to any one design formula, he had used that scheme for commercial projects since about 1870. He was certainly a major contributor to its use for high-rise buildings. Sited on Broadway near Trinity Church, the Union Trust Building, with its steep pyramidal roof and vertical design emphasis, foreshadowed the tower-skyscrapers yet to come. Broad arches at the second- and third-floor levels indicated the presence of a galleried banking hall inside. Above the banking hall's skylight, a court provided natural light and air for the interior offices.

The Union Trust Building's granite exterior walls were bearing, although the nearby Tower Building (1888–89) by Bradford Gilbert had already utilized full skeleton framing. However, in 1889 Post designed the World Building with cage framing, a type of metal construction he thought safer than skeleton framing. In cage framing, iron-framed walls support the ends of the floor beams, as distinguished from skeleton framing in which the outer walls function as non-supporting curtain walls. Post was also concerned about the vulnerability of wrought iron and steel to corrosion, and he recommended using cast-iron columns in cage construction.[24]

The opportunity for Post to design the World, or Pulitzer, Building (1889–90) must have been irresistible (fig. 41). Hunt was the professional adviser for the competition, a circumstance that may have increased Post's chances of winning the commission. Post, however, was said to have won because he boldly visited the newspaper's owner Joseph Pulitzer just after submitting his plans; he daringly "annexed" the approach to the Brooklyn Bridge by "throwing his building out over it"; and instead of guaranteeing that he could stay within the one-million-dollar budget, he made a bet with Pulitzer—twenty thousand dollars against Pulitzer's ten thousand dollars—that he could do it. That was a bet he lost.[25]

Rising about 309 feet above the sidewalk, the twenty-story World Building was at that time the tallest skyscraper ever built in New York City. Post's engineering staff was in charge of construction. The design concept was that of a multilevel Renaissance palazzo topped by a domed temple. Reportedly, the conspicuous gilded dome was Pulitzer's idea: from his private office on its second floor he could overlook the quarters of his rivals. Classicizing figural sculpture adorned the red sandstone and buff-colored

39. New York Times Building (1888–89), at center. As seen from the northwest, c.1900. Collection of the New-York Historical Society.

*40. Union Trust
Building,
New York City
(1889–90; demol-
ished). Elevation
drawing. Collection
of the New-York
Historical Society.*

*41. World (Pulitzer)
Building,
New York City
(1889–90; demol-
ished). Collection
of the New-York
Historical Society.*

*42. Collis P.
Huntington
Mansion,
New York City
(1889–94;
demolished).
Photograph of
Hughson Hawley's
perspective rendering.
Collection of
the New-York
Historical Society.*

43. Collis P. Huntington Mansion. Perspective drawing of music room. Collection of the New-York Historical Society.

82

44. Collis P.
Huntington
Mansion. Dining
room. Collection of
the New-York
Historical Society.

brick and terra-cotta walls. Karl Bitter's bronze torchbearers mounted above the entrance were intended to symbolize the arts, and four black copper atlantes beneath the pediment represented the human races. Bitter, a recent emigrant from Austria who would become one of the nation's best-known architectural sculptors, was henceforth frequently employed to work on Post's buildings. Hunt, who quickly appreciated Bitter's talent, probably drew Post's attention to him. Not surprisingly, the critics were scathing in their assessment of the building, but at least one hinted that Post was not entirely to blame for its faults. Pulitzer wanted a monument, and he got one.[26]

Another Fifth Avenue mansion came Post's way at the end of the decade. The wealthy railroad builder Collis Potter Huntington commissioned him to design a Fifth Avenue mansion (1889–94) for a site diagonally opposite the Cornelius Vanderbilt house at the southeast corner of East 57th Street (fig. 42). The two mansions were very different. Huntington's, distinguished chiefly by its rusticated stone exterior and broad, arched entranceway, was severely plain and palazzolike in contrast to Vanderbilt's chateau. Richard Morris Hunt seems to have been considered for this project first, but he was away when Mr. and Mrs. Huntington were looking around for an architect, and his assistant was said to have "bungled in his interviews."[27] Instead, Post was hired. After Hunt returned, the Huntingtons consulted him because they were dissatisfied with Post's plans, but their efforts to involve him at that point were unsuccessful. According to the Hunt papers,

> Richard, with the loyalty which characterized all his relations with his brother architects, refused to have anything to do with the work and strongly advised them to let Mr. Post try again, as their complaint was (only) that Mr. Post's original plans were too large.[28]

The Huntingtons probably requested a restrained exterior, preferring to turn their sights inward to elegantly decorated interiors (figs. 43–45). A curving marble and onyx staircase crafted by Ellin & Kitson and a large hall—actually an interior court surrounded by balconies and with a domical, sky-lighted ceiling—were two of many extraordinary features. Once again, Post worked with first-rate artists. Among them were Karl Bitter, who contributed the relief carvings, and Elihu Vedder, whose murals decorated the dining room. Edwin Howland Blashfield, whose work Post admired and whose career he helped to advance, painted the drawing room ceiling and panels. In Sturgis's opinion, "No interior of modern times seems more harmonious—more appropriate and rational as well as sumptuous in its ornamentation."[29] In the 1920s, along with the Vanderbilt mansions, the Huntington mansion yielded to the commercial redevelopment of Fifth Avenue.

CHAPTER 3

THE 1890s
Post at the Top of His Profession

The 1890s were the peak years of Post's career. His firm's many commissions ranged from skyscrapers to country houses, and included the monumental Manufactures and Liberal Arts Building at the World's Columbian Exposition as well as the Bronx Borough Hall. In the course of the decade, Post also rose to prominence as a leader in his profession. From 1893 to 1897, he was president of the Architectural League in New York; from 1896 to 1898, president of the American Institute of Architects; and from 1898 to 1905, president of the National Arts Club. By 1894, he was actively advocating a height limit for the New York skyscraper, and his efforts to that end would continue. In the midst of this activity, Post still found the time to serve as consulting architect for the Metropolitan Museum of Art after Hunt's death, and to put forward grand schemes for monumental civic and cultural buildings. In 1897 he won the competition for the new campus of the City College of New York over seven other architects, but the plans were later changed, and construction did not begin until 1903. He was said to have been so busy in 1899 that he had to resign from his position on the Board of Examiners for the New York City Buildings Department.[1] By the end of the century, his office staff numbered no fewer than sixty[2] (fig. 46).

From the time it opened, Post's Erie County Savings Bank (1890–93) in Buffalo, New York, was recognized as Richardsonian Romanesque because of its rounded corners and turrets, rock-faced sandstone masonry, and arches linking four stories (figs. 47 and 48). Post, however, had used the four-story arches in the Produce Exchange, but not the obviously Richardsonian medievalizing motifs. This combination bank–office building was planned to fit its triangular site, with wings above a two-story base.

46. "Part of Office Workforce—Office of Geo. B. Post." From Architectural Record *10 (1900).*

*47. Erie County
Savings Bank,
Buffalo, New York
(1890–93; demol-
ished). Photograph
of rendering.
Collection of
the New-York
Historical Society.*

48. Erie County
Savings Bank.
Private collection.

Post won the commission in a competition that attracted eighteen architects, most of whom were from Buffalo, but the New York firm of McKim, Mead & White also competed. Hunt was a member of the jury, and Post was the unanimous choice. Winston Weisman, who considered Post's building a "highly successful solution" to the irregularly shaped site, quipped that although the savings bank looked like a fortress, "it was no match for the demolition ball when it was destroyed several years ago [1967]."[3]

The same style also worked effectively for the first building (1890–92) of Post's Prudential Insurance Company complex in Newark, New Jersey (fig. 49). What better image for an insurance company than that of a fortress? According to *The Prudential*, five "leading architects" had submitted drawings, and Post's were judged the best. Post himself claimed that his design was "the finest piece of work he . . . [had] yet produced."[4] The company, which owned a large piece of land, expected to add buildings as needed, and accordingly, Post produced a comprehensive plan that would determine his later additions. The company was pleased that its new fireproof, twelve-story Prudential Building (later known as the Main Building) would be twice as tall as the surrounding structures, command a panoramic view from the top floors, and include a large, second-floor business hall. Post was quoted at some length on his intentions:

> This building, towering as it will above the whole city of Newark, will be the first object that meets the eye as the city is approached; and I have, therefore, attempted to so design it that it should not only be a complete and elegant mass as seen from the street, but a complete design as seen above the roofs of the adjoining houses.[5]

As expected, Post was chosen as the architect of compatible "Romanesque Gothic" additions made later on. Gothic additions to what began as Romanesque may seem odd, but he had recently undertaken to design the City College of New York campus in the Gothic style, and it may be that he wanted to signal that these were later additions. As usual, Post lavished attention on every detail, including the design of the Gothic-hooded public fountain that was set into the rounded corner of the Main Building in 1902 (fig. 50). The Broad Street fronts of Post's Main Building and his projected North Building may be seen in his proposal of about 1899 for a striking campanilelike tower adjoining a Gothic-style addition to the Main Building, and typical floor plans of about 1909 disclose the large size and intricate planning of the companion buildings fronting on Broad Street[6] (figs. 51 and 52).

Neither the tower nor the Gothic addition was built, but the Main Building was enlarged in 1899–1903, and at the same time, the North, West, and

*50. Prudential
Building.
Detail of corner
with fountain.
Collection of
the New-York
Historical Society.*

*51. Block plan
of Prudential
Insurance
Company buildings
with typical floor
plans (c. 1909).
Collection of
the New-York
Historical Society.*

*52 (opposite).
Proposed tower
for Prudential
Insurance Company
complex (c.1899).
Photograph
of rendering.
Collection of
the New-York
Historical Society.*

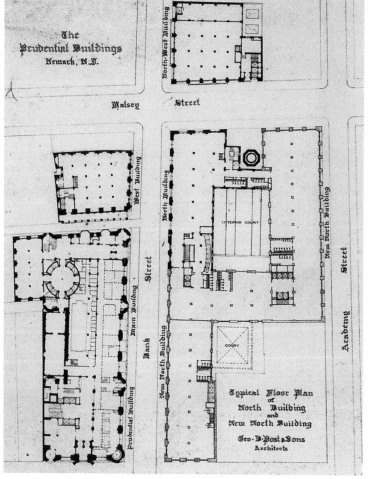

Northwest buildings were constructed. An addition to the North Building was made in 1909–13. Post's complex also included a powerhouse. As usual with Post's buildings, the interiors were embellished with art and sculpture. A statue of the founder, John F. Dryden, stood in the rotunda of Prudential's Main Building; the board room, also in the Main Building, was decorated with murals by Edwin Blashfield and others; and the assembly hall in the North Building had a Gothic pendant-vaulted ceiling. But none of this could save Post's complex from being destroyed. In addition, parts of it were altered. In 1926, the Northwest Building was replaced by Cass Gilbert's Gibraltar Building. Around 1960, Post's remaining buildings were demolished and afterwards replaced by Prudential's new quarters.[7]

The eight-story Schermerhorn Building (1890–91) on the northeast corner of Broadway and East 4th Street is the most impressive of several Post-designed mercantile buildings still standing in this area of New York City (pl. 19). Tripartite, arcaded, and warmly colorful, with red sandstone and tawny brick facades embellished with terra-cotta ornament, this structure was built for F. August Schermerhorn to house retail shops. It was restored and adapted between 1990 and 1992 to serve as the headquarters of the National Audubon Society. The original grille is still in place above the entrance, as is the row of laughing gargoyles mounted beneath the cornice. Post had developed a predilection for figural sculpture, and when the budget permitted, he typically included it. Sturgis was critical of the placement of figures high up on Post's buildings where they would be hard to see from street level, calling it "inexplicable."[8] Nevertheless, there is no more delightful experience than discovering them, and Post surely knew that the occupants of the upper floors of nearby buildings would be able to see them from their windows.

Post was one of five nonresident architects selected by Daniel Burnham to design buildings for the Chicago World's Columbian Exposition of 1893. Hunt was also one of the invited five, but at first declined to be involved due to the fact that frequent attacks of gout were taking their toll on him. Post, however, convinced Hunt to participate by telling him that "none of the New York architects would serve unless he would be at their head."[9] Perhaps as a result of Post's kindly intervention, Hunt designed the Administration Building, which stood at the head of the Court of Honor. Burnham and Post would continue their association and friendship as co-officers of the American Institute of Architects. Post served as first vice president during Burnham's term as president, and then succeeded him as president in 1896.

Post's contribution to the exposition was the enormous Manufactures and

Liberal Arts Building (1891–93), touted as "the largest structure on
earth"[10] (figs. 53 and 54). Its ground dimensions were variously reported;
Engineering News gave them as 1,687 by 787 feet, with the area of building
as 30.5 acres.[11] The arcading of the building's staff-clad exterior recalled
Post's early work, and he was obviously again inspired by the Palais de
l'Industrie from the Paris Exposition of 1855 (fig. 16). Karl Bitter was
responsible for the figural reliefs at the entrances, and the murals within
were painted by Edwin Blashfield, Kenyon Cox, J. Alden Weir, Francis D.
Millet, and other outstanding painters of the time. Post insisted on having
murals in the building, although they were said to have been opposed
because they were not really necessary. He was rightly recognized as a
leading supporter of mural painting.[12]

Post's plans were changed several times before his building was constructed. Following a general scheme first proposed by Burnham's partner
John Wellborn Root, the plans initially called for two large interior courts
surrounded by parallel exhibition galleries. Root's successor, Charles B.
Atwood, working with Edward C. Shankland, chief construction engineer
for the fair, was instrumental in causing the design to be radically
changed. The courts were omitted, and instead, a vast central hall
spanned by steel trusses was constructed (fig. 55). The intention was to
exceed the clear span of the Galerie des Machines at the Paris Exposition
of 1889, which held the record at the time. Given his past experience, his
interest in engineering problems, and his professional prominence, Post
was surely consulted on this structure even if his engineering staff did not
design the trusswork; Shankland was responsible for that. The resulting
span of 368 feet, rising to a height of 211 feet and made possible by the
largest steel trusses ever manufactured, surpassed the span of the Galerie
des Machines by three feet ten inches.[13] That difference, however small it
may seem, was indeed enough to make the Manufactures and Liberal Arts
Building the record breaker.

Post's Havemeyer Building (1891–93) was one of New York City's most
beautiful commercial buildings (figs. 56 and 57). The client was Theodore
A. Havemeyer of the famous sugar-refining family, and Post was said to
have taken "manifest delight in the task that lay before him."[14] That task
involved anticipating and coping with foundation problems and an irregularly dimensioned site in lower Manhattan. As completed, the Havemeyer
Building was a fifteen-story, cage-framed slab extending the full length
of its Church Street block between Dey and Cortlandt streets, with its
hydraulic elevator shafts contained within a semicircular extension at the
rear. For the facades, Post rejuvenated the style of the Produce Exchange
by adopting the tripartite base-shaft-capital composition of his Union Trust

53. Manufactures and Liberal Arts Building, World's Columbian Exposition, Chicago (1891–93; demolished). Photograph of E. Eldon Deane's rendering. Collection of the New-York Historical Society.

54. World's Columbian Exposition, Chicago (1893). Ground plan. From Shepp's World's Fair Photographed *(1893).*

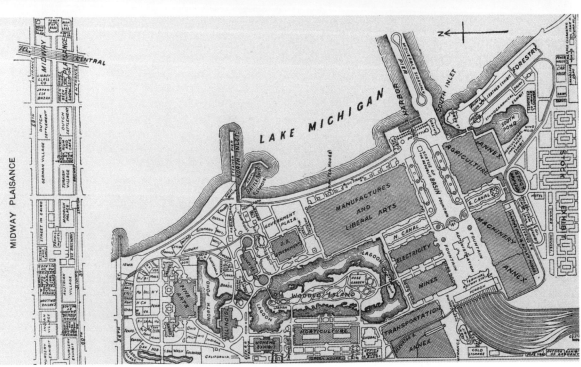

55. Manufactures and Liberal Arts Building. General interior view. From Shepp's World's Fair Photographed *(1893).*

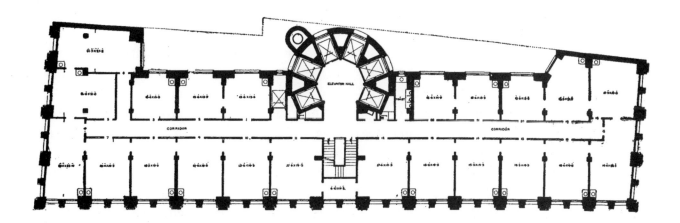

and Prudential buildings and applying classical details. The narrowness of the Dey and Cortlandt street facades probably inspired the design scheme. Light-colored brick walls were trimmed in matching limestone and terra cotta, and an impressive terra-cotta frieze with atlantes appeared to support a heavy classical cornice. As he often did in these years, Post engaged the Perth Amboy Terra Cotta Company to handle the terra-cotta ornament. Inside, on the ground floor, there was an arcade with stores and on the roof of the building, a large garden with restaurant service.[15]

Two important Pittsburgh commissions came to Post in the mid-1890s, the Bank of Pittsburgh and the Park Building. Fortunately, the Park Building (1895–96) is still standing, although many of its decorative details were removed in the 1960s (fig. 58). Its features echo those of the Havemeyer Building, including the frieze with kneeling terra-cotta atlantes (which does survive), but its taller proportions and U-shaped plan are quite different. Originally, the atlantes frieze was polychromed. The Park Building was financed by Pittsburgh steel manufacturer David Edgar Park in collaboration with his brother William G. Park, and Post's design was selected over those of five other competitors.[16] Post would seem to have overcome his concerns about steel corrosion; but judging from certain variations known to have been introduced in the skeleton of his St. Paul Building of 1895–98, he took whatever precautions he could.

56 (opposite). Havemeyer Building, New York City (1891–93; demolished). Photograph of Hughson Hawley's rendering. Collection of the New-York Historical Society.

57. Havemeyer Building. Typical floor plan. From W. H. Birkmire, Skeleton Construction in Buildings (1893; 1912 ed.).

The Bank of Pittsburgh (1895) was an updated, Beaux-Arts version of the Williamsburgh Savings Bank, with a high, stepped roof and a Roman-Corinthian portico (figs. 59 and 60). Post's training with Hunt, and his long-standing predilection for classicizing Renaissance forms, had prepared him well for the Beaux-Arts classicism of the 1890s, and this bank was an early and impressive essay in that mode. Karl Bitter was responsible for the pediment sculpture, and an extensive mural program by Blashfield decorated the interior of the domed, skylighted banking hall.[17] Unfortunately, the bank failed in the Great Depression, and all but the facade was demolished in 1944. The facade eventually yielded to a parking garage, but its columns and main doorway were saved. Since about 1960, the columns have formed the circular colonnade of the Thomas Jefferson Garden Mausoleum in the Jefferson Memorial Park cemetery in Pleasant Hills, south of Pittsburgh. The doorway frames the mausoleum gates.[18]

Post's palazzolike Bronx Borough Hall (1895–97; addition, 1898), which stood on a bluff in Crotona Park at the intersection of Tremont and Third avenues (fig. 61), reinstated the "modified Italian Renaissance" mode of his Produce Exchange. Sturgis thought it "far more reasonable and judicious in its arrangement and architectural scheme than such buildings usually are."[19] Even so, after the Bronx County Building was erected on Grand Concourse and 161st Street in 1934, Post's building gradually fell into disuse. Efforts were made to have it adapted to other purposes, but not soon enough. It was severely damaged by fire and then demolished in the late 1960s. Only the steps that led up to it survive.[20]

Post's mercantile buildings have fared better. He designed another Havemeyer Building (1895–97), this one for Theodore Havemeyer's brother, the art collector and American Sugar Refining Company president Henry Osborne Havemeyer. At 568–578 Broadway (within what was officially landmarked in 1973 as the SoHo–Cast Iron Historic District), this twelve-story building, consisting of stores and lofts, has retained its original iron grilles and spandrel reliefs. Post's fourteen-story Weld Building (1895–97; enlarged 1898) at the southwest corner of Broadway and East 12th Street is another survivor (fig. 62). The tripartite design scheme of this narrow-fronted, irregularly shaped building resembles that of the first Havemeyer and Park buildings, but its tall brick piers are pointed in profile and banded at the sill levels.[21] Post's Coe Estate Building (1896–97) at 636–638 Broadway, originally ten stories high, is similarly articulated.

At 315 feet in height, and with twenty-six stories, the St. Paul Building (1895–98) was at the time the tallest skyscraper in New York City (fig. 63). It was also commissioned by H. O. Havemeyer. While it was under

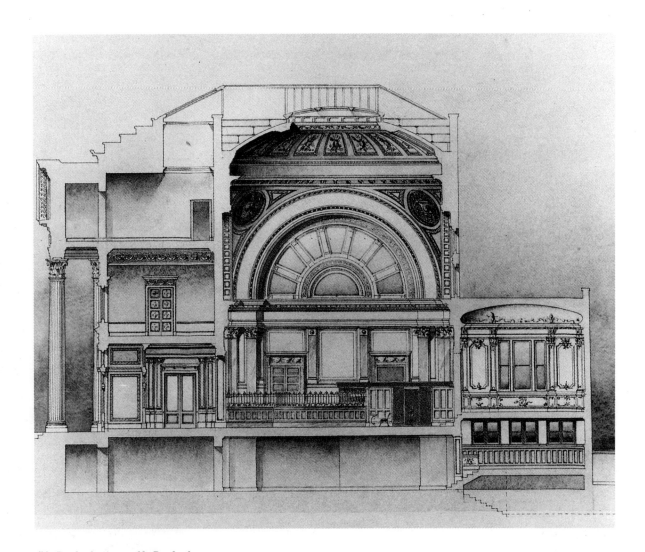

*59. Bank of
Pittsburgh (1895;
demolished).
Photograph of
rendering (1894).
Collection of
the New-York
Historical Society.*

*60. Bank of
Pittsburgh.
Preliminary section
drawing. Collection
of the New-York
Historical Society.*

61. Bronx Borough Hall, New York City (1895–97; addition, 1898; demolished). Collection of the New-York Historical Society.

*62. Weld Building,
New York City
(1895–97;
enlarged 1898).
Collection of
the New-York
Historical Society.*

*63. St. Paul
Building,
New York City
(1895–98;
demolished).
Collection of
the New-York
Historical Society.*

construction, Post was actively supporting legislation to limit building heights. At a meeting of the New York chapter of the American Institute of Architects held on March 30, 1896, he stated his views persuasively and at some length:

> I have built many of the high buildings in New York, and have on my table, at the present time, plans for several proposed new buildings in which my clients demand that they should be, in my opinion, abnormally high. I, nevertheless, believe it my duty as a citizen . . . to advocate as strongly as possible the passage of a law restricting the height of buildings . . . Our narrow streets, when lined with tall structures, will become unhealthy alleys with an inadequate capacity for the passage of the crowds which will flow from these tall buildings if occupied, for the capacity of the streets is already severely taxed at certain times of day.

Post believed that height limitation was also aesthetically justified, for even if the facade were well designed, the sides and the rear "will always form a hideous mass."[22] Noting that the St. Paul Building had given Post "the occasion to say 'I told you so' at his own expense," the *Real Estate Record and Builders Guide* saluted "the public spirit of the architect who urges that he shall be cut off from one of the most tempting avenues of professional employment."[23]

In spite of these misgivings, the impact of the St. Paul Building on surrounding buildings was relatively slight, owing to its irregularly shaped site at Broadway, Park Row, and Ann Street, opposite its namesake, the historic St. Paul's Chapel. Also, Post designed it so that the rear portion was four stories lower than the Broadway side and set back at the nineteenth floor by about twenty feet on the Ann Street side. The arrangement anticipated the setback requirements of the zoning law passed in 1916, which would finally regulate building heights in New York City. The skeleton frame was designed so as to prevent possible corrosion of the steel members and fire damage, and Post also utilized a special system of wind bracing that had been developed in Chicago.

The St. Paul Building's horizontal design scheme was mercilessly criticized, especially by Schuyler, who thought that it denied the natural similarity of the stories. Post, however, was attempting to unify three very different elevations by adopting a modular system linking the stories in pairs.[24] The building's repeated classical order and limestone cladding may have been intended to relate to the porch of St. Paul's Chapel across Broadway and also to the pilastered and columned facades of the older adjacent buildings, including the Post Office building and City Hall. By the standards of the late twentieth century, the St. Paul Building might be considered contextual, but no one would call it a "background" building.

64. St. Paul Building. Main entrance, with atlantes by Karl Bitter. Collection of the New-York Historical Society.

Its sculptural program included three kneeling atlantes, representing the principal human races, above the main entrance on Broadway (fig. 64). Again, Karl Bitter was the sculptor. The projecting ledge was later removed and replaced by consoles, making the limestone figures more visible.[25] The rule for longevity of Post's buildings seems to be the taller the edifice, the shorter its life span. In 1958 the St. Paul Building was razed and immediately replaced by a nondescript skyscraper.

In his presidential address at the 1896 annual meeting of the American Institute of Architects, Post observed that the status and influence of the architect had vastly improved since the AIA was founded in 1857. The architect had become "the accepted arbiter in all matters connected with the building art," and had at last achieved "his appreciation as an artist, and the recognition of Architecture as the most enduring, exacting, and comprehensive of the fine arts." Moreover, the architect had had a tremendous influence on the arts of painting and sculpture:

> I may state without fear of contradiction that not only does the architect furnish to the painter and sculptor now, as always, his noblest opportunities (and the benefit is mutual, for without the aid of the painter and sculptor no complete work of architecture is possible), but that hardly a movement for the advancement of art in any of its branches is successfully made throughout the land in which the architects of this Institute are not the moving spirits.[26]

Certainly, Post had provided and would continue to provide the "noblest opportunities" for painters and sculptors. The following year he described architecture as "the most exact, exacting, and comprehensive of the arts," and he proposed that the AIA members ask their wealthy clients to donate money for traveling fellowships for young architects.[27]

Since 1875, the AIA had been trying to encourage the government to hold competitions for the more important government buildings rather than have them all produced in the office of the supervising architect of the U.S. Treasury. The Tarsney Act, passed in 1893 largely due to the efforts of Daniel Burnham, and also actively supported by Hunt, authorized the supervising architect to hold invited competitions for government buildings to be juried by outside architects—but only at the discretion of the person occupying that position. During his two-year term as AIA president, Post's main agenda was to uphold and strengthen the Tarsney Act. Post pressed for amendments that would mandate the appointment of competent architects, either directly or through limited competitions, to design government buildings. He took it upon himself to nominate suitable competitors for such competitions; he offered the services of AIA directors and members as jurors; and, at the request of the supervising architect, he

65. Department of Justice Building. Competition rendering (1899). Collection of the New-York Historical Society.

selected a board made up of AIA members to examine candidates for that post. Some progress was made, but ironically, Post's well-intentioned efforts probably contributed to the ultimate demise of the Tarsney Act in 1912. It was repealed on the grounds that private architects were too costly and that the competition awards favored AIA members.[28]

Post himself actively sought government commissions at both the national and municipal levels, but all such projects were doomed to failure until the competition for the Wisconsin State Capitol in 1906 (see Chapter 4). He won the invited competition of 1899–1900 for the Washington, D.C., Department of Justice Building, but his Beaux-Arts project was not built due to insufficient government appropriations for construction costs[29] (fig. 65). In 1899 Post competed for the New York Custom House, but Cass Gilbert won the commission. That year Post also presented his project for a new City Hall building for New York. A grandiose mansarded and towered office building, as proposed to the Architectural League, it was to be

*66. Stronghold,
John F. Dryden
house,
Bernardsville,
New Jersey (1899).
Collection of
the New-York
Historical Society.*

constructed on an elevated terrace near the entrance to the Brooklyn Bridge. At the same time, Post proposed a grand plaza for the Manhattan end of the new East River (Williamsburg) Bridge. His interest in bridge approaches dates back to 1877 when he served on an advisory commission that reviewed proposals for the approaches to the Brooklyn Bridge. In 1903, caught up in the spirit of the City Beautiful and Progressive movements, he joined forces with the architect Henry F. Hornbostel, and the two submitted a plan to the city's Board of Estimate and Apportionment calling for a new civic center on Chambers Street. Their long-range scheme called for a forty-five-story municipal office building designed by Post in the form of a campanile, to be sited at the intersection of Chambers and Centre streets. Post's municipal office building was not to be constructed, and, surprisingly, his firm was not one of those invited to compete for the Municipal Building in 1907. McKim, Mead & White won that competition.[30] In 1908 Post competed for the central New York Post Office, losing to the McKim, Mead & White firm.

Since 1872, Post and his family had been spending their summers in Bernardsville, New Jersey, from which he frequently commuted by train to his New York office. The Posts were among the earliest of an elite group that would be attracted by the area's picturesque mountain setting and its proximity to New York and Newark. Gradually, the "Mountain" became the location of grand estates. In 1871 Post purchased the 104-acre Eliza Ballentine Farm, renaming it Claremont Farms, and over the years, he enlarged the existing farmhouse there for his family. He also altered and designed houses in the area for others. One of his earliest new houses there was a towered stone villa built near his own residence in 1886 for J. Coleman Drayton, a New York lawyer and the son-in-law of William Astor. In 1898 Post's client John F. Dryden, who was then president of the Prudential Insurance Company and later became a U.S. senator from New Jersey, purchased the Drayton house, and in 1899 Post enlarged it for him to include columned porches and a terrace (figs. 66 and 67). Stronghold, as the house was named, was built of stone quarried at the site. The view from the top of the tower was said to be spectacular.[31]

67. Stronghold, John F. Dryden house. From Architecture *1 (1900).*

68. Sarah Condit Cottage, Bernardsville, New Jersey (1899). Collection of the New-York Historical Society.

The Sarah Condit Cottage (1899) in Bernardsville was designed in the Colonial Revival style (fig. 68), possibly by Post's son William Stone Post (1866–1940), who entered his father's office in 1891. William had graduated from the Columbia School of Mines in 1890, and afterward traveled abroad for a year. His signature appears on drawings for many of the firm's Bernardsville residential commissions, and he was probably in charge of the alteration and enlargement of the Bernardsville house of Richard V. Lindabury (1902–3), Prudential's legal counsel. According to William Post's obituary, it was he who had designed the Prudential North Building, but even if that were so, he probably followed his father's instructions.[32]

On November 12, 1899, a full-page article in the *New York Press* entitled "Immense Museum Designed for New York" announced that Post had completed plans for a "museum of living history" intended to be "for the United States what the Kensington Museum is for England." The orig-

inator of the scheme was H. A. Spaulding, formerly with Tiffany &
Company, who had been working on the project for many years and who
expected to make it his life's work. Spaulding hoped the museum would
become the "Parthenon of America," and he was said to have aroused
the interest of the president of the United States (William McKinley) and
his cabinet as well as "scores of prominent and rich men, especially in
New York." As proposed, the museum resembled a state capitol building
with four wings of equal length at right angles to one another—the
Greek cross plan—projecting from a domed rotunda at the center (fig.
69). The building would "cover about nine and one-half acres of ground"
and rise on the Upper West Side of Manhattan where it would overlook
the Hudson River.[33] Labeled "America's Grandest Monument" on the
photograph of the elevation, this sensational museum would never be
constructed, but in the next century, Post would re-create it as the
Wisconsin State Capitol.

69. "America's Grandest Monument." Proposal for a "museum of living history" (1899). Photograph of rendering. Collection of the New-York Historical Society.

CHAPTER 4

THE LAST YEARS

Crowning Achievements

On November 24, 1899, less than two weeks after his visionary museum proposal was announced, Post won the invited competition for the New York Stock Exchange's new building. Over the years, the old exchange building had been altered and enlarged, but renovations would no longer suffice. To accommodate its replacement, additional property had been purchased on either side of its Broad Street site. The new building would have to be considerably larger than the old one in order to handle the increasing volume of business. In mid-1899 eight architects had been invited to compete for the project, with plans due October 16, 1899. In addition to Post, those invited were Carrère & Hastings, Robert Henderson Robertson, who had worked briefly in Post's firm in the early 1870s, George Kramer Thompson, Robert W. Gibson, Bruce Price, C. L. W. Eidlitz, and Heins & La Farge. Given his experience with banks and other types of buildings requiring large, open interior spaces, Post was ideally suited for this commission. He would also have had a clear understanding of how the exchange operated and what its needs were from his stockbroker son, George B. Post Jr., who had been an exchange member since 1888.[1] By late October of 1900, Post had completed his plans and submitted cost estimates (pl. 20). On April 30, 1901, the exchange moved out of its old building into temporary quarters in Post's Produce Exchange. Two years later, on April 22, 1903, Post's nine-story building was ceremoniously opened.[2]

Post's Beaux-Arts Broad Street facade was surely to some extent a response to the historic Greek Revival temple front of nearby Federal Hall on Wall Street. The exchange's white marble facade is distinguished by its raised temple front, where fluted Corinthian columns

70. New York Stock Exchange (1901–3), on opening day, April 22, 1903. New York Stock Exchange Archives.

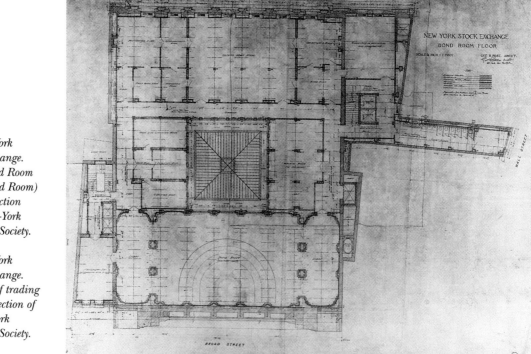

71. New York Stock Exchange. Plan, Bond Room (now Board Room) floor. Collection of the New-York Historical Society.

72. New York Stock Exchange. Drawing of trading posts. Collection of the New-York Historical Society.

backed by huge windows spanned the height of the vast trading floor, and by its allegorical pediment sculpture representing "Integrity Protecting the Works of Man" (fig. 70). Giant windows on the secondary New Street side further illuminated the trading floor. Suspended from steel girders and framed by iron mullions, these great glass walls made the grand space of the interior all the more impressive. Assisted by Paul Wayland Bartlett, John Quincy Adams Ward was responsible for the pedimental sculpture program—based on a theme determined by Post—and Getulio Piccirilli did the actual carving. Post won high praise for having once again "enlisted the services of those painters and sculptors whose work is the most powerful and effective, and whose fame he himself has done so much to perpetuate."[3]

As explained by the *Mail and Express*, "no expense had been spared," and "every possible trick of the architect has been put into play to make it [the exchange] convenient for members and their employees."[4] Schuyler had this to say regarding Post's success in designing the exchange:

> It is a distinction of Mr. Post's that he commonly manages to reduce his architectural problem to its simplest expression, to arrive at a "lay out" which recognizes the requirements according to their relative importance.

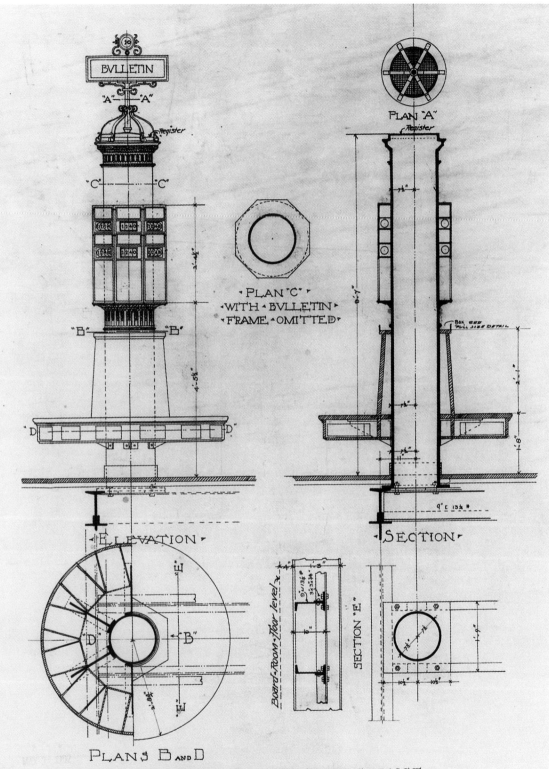

BVLLETIN

"A"——"A"

Register

"C"——"C"

"B"——"B"

D——D

· ELEVATION ·

· PLAN "A" ·
Register

· SECTION ·

Board · Room · Floor · level

SECTION "E"

PLAN "C"
· WITH · BVLLETIN ·
FRAME · OMITTED ·

PLANS B AND D

532 · NEW·YORK·STOCK·EXCHANGE ·
· DRAWING · OF · TRADING · POSTS · IN · BOARD · ROOM ·
SCALE 1"=ONE·FOOT · · ·   GEO. B. POST · ARCHITECT · · ·

Note · the · castings · to · be · made · as ·
light · as · consistant · with · reasonable ·
strength · · ·

Wood ------
Iron ------

*73. New York
Stock Exchange.
Trading floor
on opening day.
New York Stock
Exchange Archives.*

*74. New York
Stock Exchange.
Bond Room
(now Board Room)
on opening day.
New York Stock
Exchange Archives.*

> This is really one of the most important elements, one may say the most important element, of the "architectonic" equipment. It is that which Viollet le Duc, in his "Discourses" shrewdly and frankly recognizes as the great distinction of the Roman architects. It is not strictly an artistic quality, although it lies at the basis of artistic success in architecture.[5]

Like the previous Stock Exchange building, and also Post's Mills Building across the street, the new exchange extended an arm to Wall Street to make a convenient entrance there (cf. figs. 71 and 26).

The core space of the building was—and still is, though it has since been enlarged—the trading floor with its seventy-two-foot-high sky-lighted ceiling, huge window walls, and observation galleries (fig. 73). Two pairs of 115-foot-long, decoratively gilded steel trusses supported by pairs of pilasters carried the full five-thousand-ton weight of the upper stories. Large annunciator boards on the marble-paneled side walls were used to page the members, and the brokers conducted

their business at alphabetically arranged trading posts designed by
Post to include banquettes for seating (fig. 72). Aside from the
trading floor, the most important rooms were the Luncheon Club
on the seventh floor and the Board Room, originally called the Bond
Room, on the sixth floor (figs. 71 and 74). The Board Room's special
features included the decorative skylight at the center of its coffered
ceiling, paneled walls tinted "pale apple green" with inscribed arches
matching the open arches at either end of the room, and a stepped,
semicircular seating area for the Board of Governors.[6] Post was
responsible for all the details, including the design of the leather-
upholstered mahogany chairs.

In every respect the new exchange was technologically advanced. It had,
in fact, one of the earliest large, mechanical, air-cooling installations.
Knowing that the window walls would make the trading room even hotter
than it would normally be, Post contacted the prominent ventilating and

*75. Montreal
Stock Exchange
(1903–4).
Rendering as built.
Collection of
the New-York
Historical Society.*

heating engineer Alfred R. Wolff. In New York City, Wolff had already installed cooling systems at Carnegie Hall in 1889, at the Hanover National Bank in 1893, and at the Cornell Medical College in 1899. For the Stock Exchange, he devised a system (using ammonia as the refrigerant) that is considered "the largest and most scientifically designed air-conditioning system up to that time."[7]

While the New York Stock Exchange was going up, Post was commissioned to design the Montreal Stock Exchange (1903–4), and the Montreal firm of Edward & W. B. Maxwell consulted on the construction of this comparatively modest but well-proportioned building (fig. 75). It has no pediment and no figural sculpture, but Post was able to set the center trading room section back from the building line and

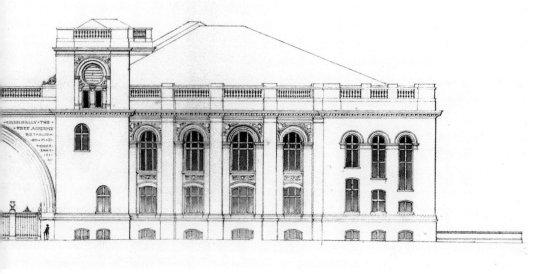

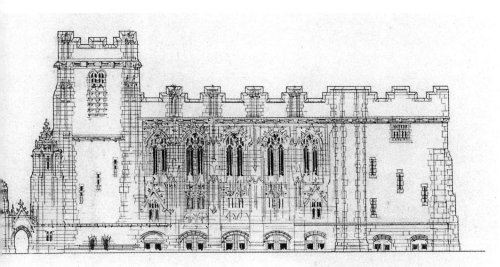

*76. City College
of New York.
Competition design
(1897) showing
Convent Avenue
elevation in
Beaux-Arts style.
Collection of
the New-York
Historical Society.*

*77. City College
of New York.
Competition design
(1897) showing
Convent Avenue
elevation in
Collegiate Gothic
style. Collection of
the New-York
Historical Society.*

frame it effectively with low projecting wings. The center section has
a row of large windows behind its Roman Corinthian colonnade. Since
about 1966, the exchange has been used as a theater.[8]

In 1897 Post had been selected as the architect of the new City College
of New York campus. The student body had long since outgrown the college's downtown quarters, and after an intensive search for an appropriate location, the trustees had purchased a site on St. Nicholas Heights
overlooking the Hudson and East rivers and much of the city. The opportunity to create a college campus on a dramatic, elevated site must have
challenged Post, who was accurately described by Sturgis as both "the
essentially picturesque designer and the determined realist."[9] However,
due to various legal and financial problems, construction did not begin

*78. Main Building,
City College of
New York.
Preliminary sketch
of St. Nicolas
Terrace side
(c.1902).
Center section not
as built. Collection
of the New-York
Historical Society.*

until 1903. As explained by Arthur Ebbs Willauer, who had been a drafts-
man in Post's office when the project was at a standstill, Post persevered,
but not without some financial loss:

> Throughout this long-drawn-out period, beset on every side by constantly
> changing and almost endless difficulties in the execution of this work, the
> architect . . . never hesitated to work for "improvement" and for the "best,"
> invariably at great personal loss. If the true story of this loss were known it
> would show a loyal tribute to the best ideals of the profession of architecture.[10]

Post had initially offered the trustees a choice between the Beaux-Arts and
Collegiate Gothic styles (figs. 76 and 77). Had they selected the former,
which Post was said to favor, he would have used the arcaded Beaux-Arts
style of his Manufactures and Liberal Arts Building, but the Gothic was

chosen for its picturesque potential. The college's original Free Academy building was Gothic Revival in style, and the Collegiate Gothic was currently in vogue for American college campuses. The trustees may have been influenced by the fact that Gothic towers on an elevated site would contrast conspicuously with the domed Beaux-Arts buildings of Columbia University and the Fordham Heights campus of New York University.

Post had first planned a campus consisting of a single large, fan-shaped building enclosing three courts separated by passages designated as "cloisters" on the plan, and with its curved side conforming to the contour of St. Nicholas Terrace.[11] However, more money was allocated for the project, and in 1902 the plans were modified to include more buildings. Main Building (Shepard Hall) was

*79. City College
of New York.
Bird's-eye view
looking southwest
(1902), showing
buildings as
constructed in
1903–7.
Collection of
the New-York
Historical Society.*

redesigned in an anchor shape with a Great Hall extending westward
from its center (figs. 78–80). As the grandest space on the campus,
with seating for 2,400 people, the Great Hall was expected to accommodate civic as well as academic functions. Heavy buttresses, large
traceried windows, twin towers containing organ lofts, and a Gothic,
beamed ceiling simulate English great halls of the late Tudor era
(fig. 81). In the stage area, a large mural by Blashfield depicts "The
Graduate" with allegorical and distinguished historical figures.

Four more Post-designed buildings were sited on a large terrace on
the west side of Convent Avenue: the Gymnasium (Wingate Hall),
Sub-Freshman (Harris Hall), Mechanical Arts (Compton Hall), and
Chemical (Baskerville Hall) buildings. Although the overall scheme
is formal and might even be characterized as neoclassical in concept,

the individual buildings are differently treated within the formal terrace grouping. The most eye-catching of the group is the Mechanical
Arts Building. Although its Gothic details harmonize with those of the
surrounding buildings, it was intentionally given a factorylike appearance to express its functions, which included housing the campus
power plant in the basement. Instead of trying to disguise the necessary tall chimney, Post boldly "place[d] this stack in the most conspicuous place in the building and [made] an ornamental feature of it"[12]
(pl. 21). The building's two principal floors are bracketed by piers and
tall segmental arches in a Gothic variation on a favorite Post motif.
Also of interest is the faintly outlined structure behind the Mechanical
Arts Building seen in the bird's-eye view of the campus (fig. 79).
Apparently, another building in this location was anticipated early on,
and in 1929–30 the School of Technology building (now Goethals

*80. City College
of New York.
View of 138th
Street gate and
Main Building
(Shepard Hall).
Collection of
the New-York
Historical Society.*

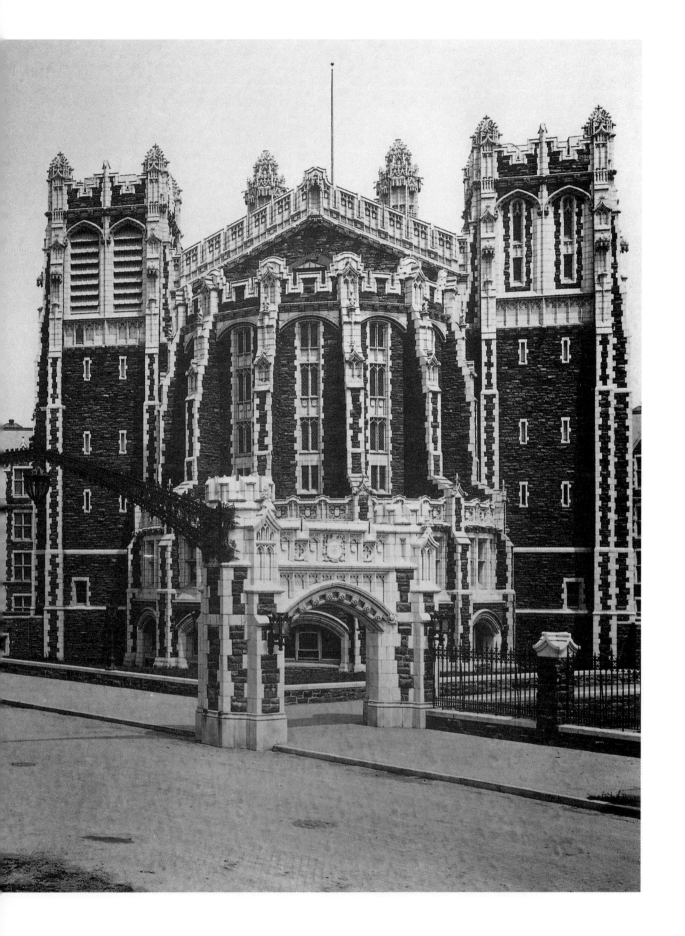

*81. City College
of New York.
Interior of Great
Hall. Collection
of the New-York
Historical Society.*

Hall), designed by Post's successor firm, was built on that site. Although compatibly styled, Goethals Hall is rather plain in comparison to Post's richly ornamented buildings.[13]

St. Nicolas Terrace is a steep ridge of rock of the type known as Manhattan schist. Extensive blasting and excavating were required to accommodate the foundations of the new buildings and an underground passageway connecting them. To offset the high cost of this procedure, the rock that was excavated was used for the walls of the buildings; and to vary the gray color, "great care was used (much to the disgust of the Italian masons on the work) to have as many as possible of the rusty and iron-touched stones show in the stonework."[14] Manufactured by the Perth Amboy Terra Cotta Company, white terra cotta was used to trim the dark, occasionally rust-stained, stone walls and also for the sculptural decoration (fig. 80). This color scheme was much criticized at the time, especially by Schuyler, who admired the buildings but found the contrast of materials and colors violent and disturbing.[15] Few today would agree with that negative judgment; in fact, the color contrast and the subtle rust spotting in the stonework are quite effective.

The sculpture was intended to express the particular purpose of each building, and to that end, more than six hundred designs for cornice grotesques were made (fig. 82). Post took a personal interest in every detail. He was said to have made the drawings for the grotesques himself, but the artist was Livingston Smith, a member of his staff.[16] An engaging photograph shows Post standing between two statues of lions—looking rather like a lion himself—in a workroom at the Perth Amboy Terra Cotta Company where he had gone to correct the models for the sculpture (fig. 83). The lions would be mounted above the entrance to the Gymnasium building. It was Post's habit to visit regularly the studios of artists working on his projects, and he made those visits because he believed the architect should have full control over the final result:

> The only way in which a satisfactory result can be obtained is to have the
> model made under constant criticism and inspection of the architects, and
> to have it altered and changed until it has the spirit which the full size
> drawing was intended to convey.[17]

Other Post essays in the Gothic style include the Bernardsville house he designed for his son George B. Post Jr. Named Kenilwood (1903–4), the residence was actually a thorough renovation of an existing house (fig. 84). Except for the color of its stone walls, it would have fit in comfortably with the City College buildings. In 1904 Post's project for a Collegiate Gothic

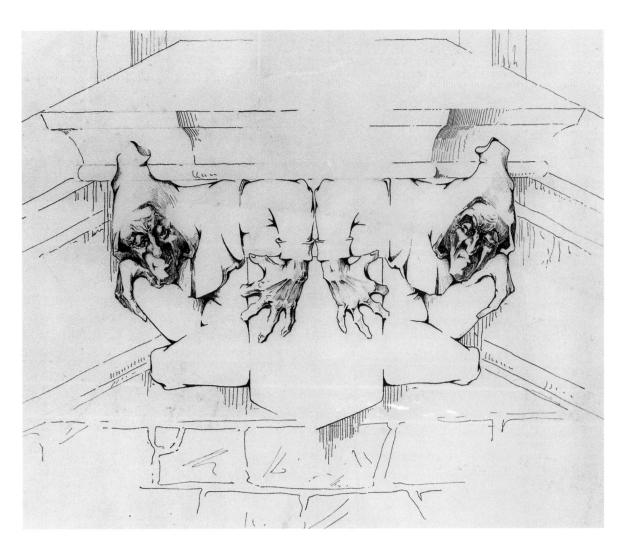

*82. Main Building,
City College of
New York. "Special
figure at High
Point, Gable—End
of Great Hall."
Collection of
the New-York
Historical Society.*

*83. Post correcting
models for City
College at Perth
Amboy Terra Cotta
Company.
Collection of
the New-York
Historical Society.*

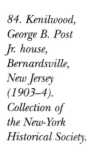

84. Kenilwood,
George B. Post
Jr. house,
Bernardsville,
New Jersey
(1903–4).
Collection of
the New-York
Historical Society.

85. Claremont, George B. Post house, Bernards-ville, New Jersey (1904–5). Collection of the New-York Historical Society.

campus for Carnegie Technical Schools of Pittsburgh won second place in a competition.[18] But in the case of his own new Bernardsville house, known as Claremont (1904–5), Post opted for the currently popular Neo-Federal style—perhaps because it permitted a more formal parti than the Gothic would have (fig. 85). The Palladian-arched porte cochere at the north, entrance front was matched on the south, garden facade by a curving portico similar to the one on the terrace end of the Dryden house, Stronghold. From this portico, the owners have a remarkable sweeping view down the mountainside. Inside Claremont, a central grand staircase leads to the second floor, where the bedroom–sitting room suites are located, and affords a fine view from its garden-side stair landing. The porte cochere has been removed; fortunately, a pair of lion sculptures remains near the entrance as a reminder of the architect who designed and lived in the house.[19]

In 1904 Post changed his firm's name from George B. Post to George B. Post & Sons. A second son, James Otis Post (1873–1951), had entered his office in 1901. James had just qualified for a diploma from the Ecole des Beaux-Arts, where he had been studying since his graduation from Columbia in 1896. In 1902 he tried practicing independently, but by 1904 was back in his father's office, and he and his brother William were then made full partners in the firm (fig. 86). From this point on, the sons must be considered active participants in designing and overseeing construction of the firm's buildings. William Post, in fact, was heavily involved in making the final plans for the City College buildings.[20]

The firm's four-story Keppel Building (1904–5) at 4 East 39th Street in New York, was designed in the Gothic style with a crenellated roofline, a pair of aggressive gargoyles bracketing the cornice, windows in groups of four framed in stone, and a Tudor-arched storefront (fig. 87). The most intriguing feature of this odd little building is the pair of high-relief sculpted heads framing the storefront, Rembrandt on the left and Whistler on the right. They served to advertise discreetly and tastefully the business of the building's owner and occupant, Frederick Keppel & Company. Keppel was a respected art dealer and connoisseur who specialized in prints, particularly etchings and engravings, and who also lectured and published books on the subject. Post must have enjoyed this project.[21]

On the other hand, how frustrating it must have been for Post to have won the competition for the proposed George Washington University campus, and then not to have it built. Since 1903, discussions had been going on between Columbian University in Washington, D.C., and a group known as the George Washington Memorial Association, which wanted to establish a memorial to Washington in the form of a large and

86. Left to right: William Stone Post, George B. Post, and James Otis Post. From New York Architect 3 *(1909).*

impressive building. As a result of this alliance, plans were made to construct a memorial building with an auditorium and space for graduate study and research on university-owned property in Washington's Van Ness Park, and the name of the university was changed from Columbian to George Washington. A competition was held in 1905, and Post's firm submitted an ambitious plan that, optimally, would have resulted in the construction of seven buildings, with a domed Memorial Hall as the most prominent (figs. 88 and 89). Appropriately, Memorial Hall would have faced in the direction of the Washington Monument; the contiguous, linked buildings would have been oriented toward President's Park and Potomac Park in an arrangement recalling that of City College. Memorial Hall would have had a deep Corinthian-columned portico, and its dome would have covered the auditorium. These plans were announced in the *Washington Post* and other newspapers with the news that construction of Memorial Hall would begin in the near future. The other buildings, it was hoped, would soon follow. However, it proved impossible to raise the half-million dollars needed for the memorial building, and the university decided that Van Ness Park was not a suitable location and sold its property. In 1909 the project was abandoned. No further attempt at a comprehensively planned campus was made until the 1920s, and the university today comprises buildings dating from the mid-nineteenth century to the 1980s.[22]

In spite of that disappointment, 1905 was a boom year for Post. His winning competition design for the Cleveland Trust Company's quarters (1905–8) was constructed as planned, giving him yet another domed, artist-decorated bank to his credit (figs. 90 and 91). Rightly described as "an ingenious solution to problems posed by an irregular site," the steel-framed, granite-sheathed exterior enclosed a tall rotunda surrounded by three floors of offices.[23] The main facades, at either side of a chamfered corner at the intersection of East 9th Street and Euclid Avenue, recall the New York Stock Exchange's Broad Street front. Karl Bitter designed the sculpture for both pediments. The one on East 9th Street displays the company's coat of arms, and the Euclid Avenue pediment represents the "mainsprings of wealth" with allegorical figures. But the glory of this building is its eighty-five-foot-high galleried rotunda surmounted by a double glass dome with delicately leaded glass and encircled at its base by electric rosette lights (fig. 92). A series of murals on the curving walls of this handsome room by Francis Millet, whose paintings had decorated the north pavilions of Post's Manufactures and Liberal Arts Building at the World's Columbian Exposition, depicts the settling of Ohio.[24]

The Cleveland Trust Company Building was by no means Post's only work

87. Keppel Building, New York City (1904–5). Photograph by author.

88. *George Washington University campus. Photograph of competition rendering (1905). Collection of the New-York Historical Society.*

89. *George Washington University campus. Photograph of competition plan (1905). Collection of the New-York Historical Society.*

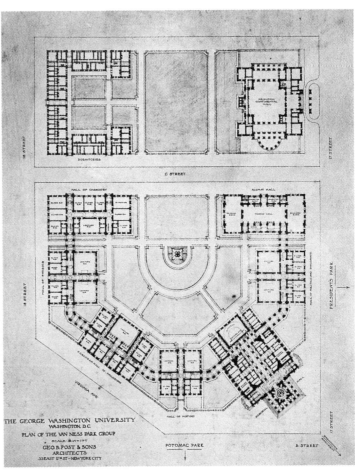

THE GEORGE WASHINGTON UNIVERSITY
WASHINGTON, D.C.
PLAN OF THE VAN NESS PARK GROUP
SCALE: 16 Ft = 1 FT
GEO. B. POST & SONS
ARCHITECTS
33 EAST 17TH ST - NEW YORK CITY

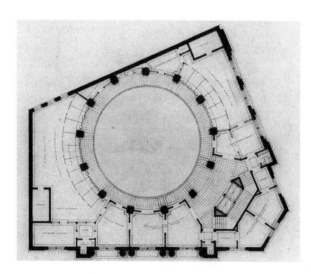

*90. Cleveland
Trust Company
Building
(1905–8). Plan
of second floor.
Collection of
the New-York
Historical Society.*

*91. Cleveland
Trust Company
Building.
Collection of
the New-York
Historical Society.*

in that city. He had previously designed the sixteen-story Williamson Building (1899–1900), and more Cleveland commissions would follow, among them the Wade Park Branch of the Cleveland Trust Company (1906–7), the Statler Hotel (1911–12), and other hotels designed by his successor firm. The Post firm maintained a branch office in Cleveland for many years. The Williamson and Wade Park Branch buildings have been razed, but the firm's Statler Hotel, and the successor firm's Mount Sinai Hospital (c.1915), Wade Park Manor (c.1922), Fenway Hall Hotel (c.1922), and National Town and Country Club (1930, now Fenn College Tower, Cleveland State University) are extant. In 1911 Post's firm was consulted on the design and construction of the Cleveland Union Terminal.[25]

92. Cleveland Trust Company Building. Rotunda. Collection of the New-York Historical Society.

While engaged with the Cleveland Trust Company Building, the Post firm was also working on a hospital commission. In 1905 the firm was commissioned to design the New Jersey State Tuberculosis Sanatorium (1905–7) in Glen Gardner, New Jersey (fig. 93). Not since his work on New York Hospital had Post handled a hospital facility, and this one would be the first of several large hospital complexes George B. Post & Sons would produce. Fresh air, rest, and a nutritious diet were then the prescribed treatment for tuberculosis, and the five-hundred-acre site of the Glen Gardner facility—on a mountain slope about 950 feet above sea level, not far from the railroad station, with a good fresh water supply, southern exposure, and "natural attractions"—was considered ideal for the open-air rest cure.[26] Both the setting and the need for screened porches probably influenced the choice of the currently popular Mission style, with its requisite tiled and hipped roofs, stuccoed walls—in this case, stuccoed fieldstone—and trellised walkways. Post's complex included a central administration building flanked by east and west wards and a service building to the rear. These were constructed so that additions could be accommodated as needed, and numerous additions have indeed been made over the years, though not by Post's firm. The original buildings, somewhat altered, form the center of what has been since 1977 the Hagedorn Gero-Psychiatric Hospital, a nursing home.

The firm's Samaritan Hospital (1912–14) in Troy, New York, is also still functioning, and its exterior is largely intact. An early rendering proposes a combination Mission- and Neo-Federal-style facade with roof trellises, a columned and towered center, and stuccoed walls (fig. 94). However, as constructed, the pavilion-plan complex is Neo-Federal with columned porticoes, wire-cut tapestry brick walls, and limestone and terra-cotta trim (figs. 95 and 96). The architect's problem, as explained by James Otis Post, was "to arrange an elastic group plan which may be capable of being built in units and later developed still farther by units . . .

93 (top).
New Jersey State
Tuberculosis
Sanatorium,
Glen Gardner,
New Jersey
(1905–7).
Collection of
the New-York
Historical Society.

94. Samaritan
Hospital, Troy,
New York
(1912–14).
Presentation
rendering (1912).
Collection of
the New-York
Historical Society.

SAMARITAN HOSPITAL
TROY N.Y.
GEO. B. POST & SONS

*95. Samaritan
Hospital.
Collection of
the New-York
Historical Society.*

96. Samaritan Hospital. Photograph of bird's-eye view (November 15, 1914). Collection of the New-York Historical Society.

The wings of the ward buildings should, if possible, be planned so as to receive the maximum sunlight from the southeast to the southwest." The style, "English Renaissance of the Georgian period," was chosen "to give to the buildings a cheerful domestic character rather than the cold formality which is commonly found in institutional buildings."[27] The complex included a nurses' home and three ward pavilions—male, female, and private—linked to a central administration building, as well as separate buildings for a servants' dormitory, a contagious disease ward, and a service and power plant. More buildings were added by Post's successor firm in 1924 and 1930. The fact that the successor firm's Mount Sinai Hospital (c.1915) in Cleveland was so similar in appearance and plan suggests that Post's sons were heavily involved with the Samaritan project.[28]

While these medical facilities were under construction, Post was working on the building that would be his last major work and the crowning achievement of his career, the Wisconsin State Capitol (1906–17). Winning the competition for this important commission enabled him to bring "America's Grandest Monument" to life. Although he did not live to see the capitol finished, he died knowing that his sons would see that it was completed as planned, and that the best artists of his time would produce its sculpture, murals, and mosaics.

It was altogether fitting that Post's career should end with a state government's "living museum," because over the years he had done much to further the arts, not only by employing sculptors and artists, but through his professional status and influence. Since 1900 Post had held high positions in various professional organizations, and his advice on important projects was constantly solicited. From its founding in 1898 to 1905, he was president of the National Arts Club, and he designed the club's Studio Building (1905–6). In 1905 the club purchased the Samuel J. Tilden residence on Gramercy Park South for its quarters, and Post's fifteen-story building was constructed behind it on East 19th Street. The ornamental grotesques and Tudor-Gothic entrance of this otherwise rather plain, brick-clad building recall the City College buildings (fig. 97). In all, there were thirty apartments, with duplex studio apartments on every other floor facing north toward Gramercy Park.[29] Hunt's Tenth Street Studio Building and his pioneering Stuyvesant Apartments (1869–70), which stood just two blocks away, were the precedents for buildings like Post's.

From 1901 to 1909, Post was a director of the Municipal Art Society of New York; he was appointed by the governor of New York State to serve on the Board of Commissions of the St. Louis Exposition in 1902; in 1904

*97. National Arts
Club Studio
Building,
New York City
(1905–6).
Detail of main
facade.
Photograph
by author.*

he became president of the New York chapter of the AIA. Post officially
represented American architects at the World's Congress of Architects
held in London in 1906, and that same year was appointed by the
Secretary of Agriculture as collaborator to the Forest Service of the U.S.
Department of Agriculture. Post was made a member of the permanent
committee of the International Congress of Architects in 1908, and the
following year President Theodore Roosevelt appointed him to the
Bureau of Fine Arts. The honors came one after the other. In 1900 Post
was awarded a silver medal at the Paris Exposition; in 1901 the French
decorated him a chevalier of the Legion of Honor; in 1907 he was
appointed honorary corresponding member of the Royal Institute of
British Architects and elected an associate of the National Academy
of Design. Post was elected an academician of the National Academy
of Design and also awarded an honorary Doctor of Laws by Columbia
University in 1908. In 1911 he received the AIA's Gold Medal. John La
Farge, who had recommended him for the honorary degree, was one
of those who spoke at the AIA's annual convention in favor of Post's

receiving the Gold Medal. The list of Post's achievements is indeed impressive. Over the course of his long career, he belonged to, or was elected to, virtually every important organization with a connection to architecture and art.[30]

Post's experience with state capitols began with his daring, though unsuccessful, competition project for the Connecticut State Capitol (see pl. 4). In 1884 he had served as adviser on the Georgia State Capitol competition, and had selected Willoughby J. Edbrooke and Franklin P. Burnham's proposal as the winner on the basis of its being "more academic in its plan than the other designs. It is very dignified and more simple & elegant in detail than that of Myers [another competitor]; less picturesque but more monumental."[31] This statement would seem to sum up his conception of what a state capitol should be, and "monumental" is certainly the appropriate adjective for his Wisconsin State Capitol.

Post's Wisconsin Capitol would replace one built in the 1860s that had been largely destroyed by fire early in 1904. An abortive competition was held in November 1904, which Post did not enter. In 1905, the state legislature ruled for a new competition, and the Madison, Wisconsin, architect Lew Porter prepared the program. Porter would also serve as Capitol Commission secretary during construction. Post's was one of five proposals submitted in the competition held during the spring of 1906; the other competitors were the Milwaukee firms of Ferry & Clas and H. C. Koch & Company and the Boston firms of Shepley, Rutan & Coolidge and Peabody & Stearns. The program prescribed a plan with four wings radiating from the central, domed section—construction of these five parts was to be phased—and one of the capitol commissioners recommended that the plan take the form of a St. Andrew's cross, in effect, a Greek cross with the wings diagonally oriented toward the corners of the square site. The opportunity actually to use the Greek-cross plan must have seemed like a dream come true for Post. The competition judges, Daniel Burnham and Lew Porter, selected his design as the best[32] (pl. 22). It fully merited Burnham's praise: "The Post design . . . shows something more than mere scholarship; it has a quality that goes with its terrace, which . . . is unusually good. This is due to the just treatment of the dome and platform through which the dome rises. This general mass is impressive and beautiful."[33]

In the statement that accompanied his competition plans, Post pointed out that his design met all the program requirements and proposed a steel-framed dome and white marble for the building's exterior—with white granite as the second choice. He also drew attention to the design's special merits, including "porch entrances at the re-entering angles of the maltese cross" in addition to entrances at the ends of the wings and "the fact that each one of the eight entrances leads toward a point of brilliant light under the center of the dome and that from each there is a continuous vista to the opposing porch." While the new dome follows "the general character of your present dome [that of the old Capitol] . . . we believe that ours possesses the merit of much greater distinctive individuality." Moreover, he explained that the four domed towers flanking the main dome would not be useless, because they "may serve as chambers for the exhaust fans."[34] And Post wanted to situate the domed center of his building at the center of the park rather than in the position of the previous capitol dome. Inspired by McKim, Mead & White's Rhode Island State Capitol (1895–1905)—and also proposed for "America's Grandest Monument"—the four towers were criticized by Burnham as being too large. In fact, they were subsequently eliminated in favor of pedestals with sculpture groups. White granite was selected for the exterior, but it was agreed that the center of the building would be at the park's center.[35]

Traditionally, state capitols were expected to possess certain fixed elements: a domed center with wings, large chambers for government functions, and impressive public hallways. For Post, the challenge was not only to accommodate those features and make his capitol beautiful in the process, but also to ensure that his building was functional and cost-efficient as well. To those ends, he planned the capitol with what appears to be a modular office system, to provide as much office space as possible. He used skylights in the main chambers and barrel vaults, glass blocks in the flooring of the second story, and sidelights and transoms in areas that otherwise would have received insufficient natural light. He positioned the ductwork so as to leave as much unencumbered floor space as possible. As projected, construction went forward section by section beginning with the west wing, which was started in the fall of 1906. The east wing was begun in 1909; the central portion, in the spring of 1910; the south wing, in December 1910; the final section, the north wing, was finished in 1917 (figs. 98 and 99). During those years, letters and telegrams from Post's firm were sent nearly every day to Porter. These document the firm's careful oversight of and interest in all aspects of the project, including such minor details as door handles and soap dishes; even the cuspidors were specially designed by the firm. Post was fully in charge and, as usual, deeply involved in the interior decoration. He visited the site twenty times from 1907 until his death in 1913.[36]

99. Wisconsin State Capitol. Collection of the New-York Historical Society.

*100. Italian
Evangelical
Church,
Bernardsville,
New Jersey
(1909–10).
Perspective
rendering.
Collection of
the New-York
Historical Society.*

All the interiors, but especially the Senate and Assembly chambers and the central rotunda, are impressive in their proportions, various and often colorful materials, and fine artistic decoration (pl. 23). Leading artists of the time, many of whom had previously worked with Post, were engaged to handle the painting and sculpture. Most of the figural artwork is allegorical, and in one way or another its themes relate to the state of Wisconsin and its government. Blashfield was responsible for the inner dome mural, which represents "The Resources of Wisconsin," and also the Assembly Chamber mural. Bitter handled the sculpture of the west- and east-wing pediments and also the pedestal sculpture groups. Kenyon Cox, whose art had decorated Post's Manufactures and Liberal Arts Building, painted the Senate Chamber mural and also did the mosaics in the dome pendentives. Other New York City artists participated; among them were Adolph A. Weinman, who was the sculptor for the south pediment, and Attilio Piccirilli, who handled the north pediment. (Piccirilli's brother had worked on the

Stock Exchange pediment.) Daniel Chester French was the sculptor of the gilded bronze figure of "Wisconsin" on top of the dome. Bitter's work, at least, was complete and in place before Post's death.[37]

On November 28, 1913, Robert R. Houston of Post's firm sent a telegram to Lew Porter informing him that George B. Post had died that day. Acknowledging Porter's return sympathy telegram, James Otis Post wrote, "Father's life & death are envied by most of us. His life so full of action & accomplishment & his death so peaceful & painless."[38] From then on, Post's sons were in complete charge of all the firm's projects. There is reason to believe that they had been responsible for several of the many commissions obtained after they became their father's partners and before his death, although Post undoubtedly provided guidance.

The designer of the Italian Evangelical (Presbyterian) Church (1909–10) in Bernardsville, however, was surely Post himself. If the preliminary rendering of this rubblestone country chapel is compared to the romantic drawing made in the 1860s at the beginning of his career, when he was Gambrill's partner, that would seem the logical conclusion (cf. figs. 100 and 1). Furthermore, Post donated the plans, and the Basking Ridge Presbyterian Church, his own parish church, paid for most of the construction. Italians had started coming to Bernardsville after the Civil War to work on roads and railroad tracks; skilled workers came to construct and care for the estates; and by the turn of the century, Italians were a substantial presence in the village. Although long ago outgrown by its congregation, the former Italian Evangelical Church survives as a private residence.[39]

An article describing a festive dinner given in 1897 by the Architectural League in Post's honor had this to say about his work, with reference to his Manufactures and Liberal Arts Building: "This colossal structure, the largest of the kind ever constructed, was perhaps typical of Mr. Post's general work: big, well adapted to utilitarian needs, and possessing a large measure of dignity."[40] That statement also characterizes his legacy to his sons (fig. 101). Although finished in 1912, the Hotel Statler in Cleveland was their project, and the firm's Pontiac Hotel (1910–12) in Oswego, New York, was likely also theirs. The firm, however, had gotten those jobs because of Post's reputation and architecture. No architect had "contributed more to the solution of the architectural problems of his generation" than Post.[41] Using the resources bequeathed by Post, that "most exact, exacting, and comprehensive" of architects, James Otis Post and William Stone Post moved the firm resolutely into twentieth-century corporate design.

101. George B. Post & Sons drafting room, 101 Park Avenue, New York City, c.1913. Collection of the New-York Historical Society.

THE SUCCESSOR FIRM

P ost had absolute confidence in his sons: "It would be difficult to find two more able Architects than my two partners and they are thoroughly competent in every way to take charge of the [Wisconsin State Capitol] entire building."[1] He died secure in the knowledge that they would not only keep the firm alive, but keep it active. In fact, George B. Post & Sons had a New York City office in the Architects Building at 101 Park Avenue until 1972, although William Stone Post had retired in 1930, and James Otis Post died in 1951. Edward Everett Post, James's son, joined the firm in 1946 and became its principal in 1949. Under his direction, the office of George B. Post & Sons was located in Huntington, Long Island, from 1972 to 1995. At the time of James Otis Post's death in 1951, the Post firm had executed projects "aggregating more than $170,000,000" since 1904.[2] Its major work had been hotels.

Although the firm was not the architect of the first Statler hotel, which was built in Buffalo in 1907–8, it was responsible for the second, third, and fourth, in Cleveland (1911–12), Detroit (1914–15), and St. Louis (1917), respectively (figs. 102 and 103). The firm also designed the second Buffalo Statler (1921–23) and the Boston Statler (1926–27). The firm of Mauran, Russell & Crowell collaborated on the St. Louis Statler, which, when it opened in 1917, was criticized for being a "carbon copy of the previous Statler houses."[3] Certainly, the Cleveland Statler established precedents for the ones that followed, including the Statler style, "a mélange of the Italian Renaissance and the English [Robert] Adam" said to have "met with instant favor from the profession and the public." Murals and Adamesque ceiling plasterwork decorated the principal public spaces, and a "studied similarity" in the rooms and their arrangement gave the Statler hotels the desired

102. Statler Hotel, Cleveland (1911–12). George B. Post & Sons, architects. From Architectural Record 36 (1914).

176

103. Statler Hotel,
St. Louis (1917).
George B. Post
& Sons, architects.
Private collection.

"striking family resemblance."[4] A newspaper article about the Cleveland
Statler's grand opening includes a photograph of the "Men Behind the
Statler," showing James and William Post seated at the center with E. M.
Statler, founder of the chain, standing between them.[5]

The firm designed many other hotels, including the Roosevelt (1922–24)
and the Warwick (1925–27) in New York City. The huge Roosevelt Hotel
established the cost-effective practice of having shops on the ground floors
of hotels.[6] The Warwick was built as a thirty-six-story apartment hotel by
William Randolph Hearst, but from the beginning it also catered to out-of-
town visitors (fig. 104). It was later converted into a regular hotel with five
hundred rooms. Its U-shaped plan can be traced to George B. Post and his
Post Building, though not the setbacks, which were mandated by the 1916
zoning law. The firm also collaborated on the Hearst Magazine Building
(1927–28), designed by the Viennese-born and -trained Joseph Urban. This
impressive six-story building was expected to become the base of a twenty-
story skyscraper. In 1946 the Post firm proposed a nine-story addition to rise
from that base, but it was never built.[7]

104. Warwick Hotel, New York City (1925–27). George B. Post & Sons, architects. Perspective rendering (1925) by W. S. Wagner. Collection of the New-York Historical Society.

The successor firm also designed housing projects, the first being the garden village of Eclipse Park (1917–18) in Beloit, Wisconsin. That commission was secured because George B. Post & Sons was known to be the architect of the Wisconsin State Capitol. By the time Eclipse Park was proposed during World War I, there were about 230 such projects in the United States, many of them employers' housing for workers. Fairbanks, Morse & Company, formerly known as the Eclipse Windmill Company, the manufacturer of internal combustion engines and steam pumps, expected the war to increase its volume of business. It had hired a thousand new workers, and wanted to provide them with reasonably priced housing on terms they could afford. The site chosen, adjoining the company's athletic field on the south side, was within walking distance of the factory and bordered the Rock River on its west side. At first, the plan was to extend the existing grid pattern of streets into that fifty-acre area, but the Post firm convinced the company that such a scheme would be "more expensive than a contour plan which the rolling character of a large part of the tract favored . . . in the new scheme streets were designed for local use only"[8] (fig. 105). The narrow, curving streets, along with varied lot sizes and house types, were

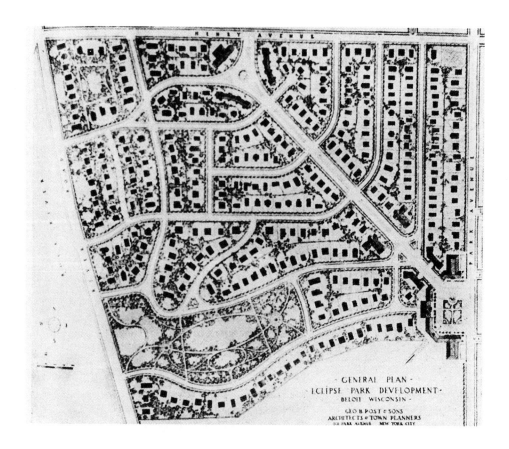

105. Eclipse Park Development, Beloit, Wisconsin (1917). George B. Post & Sons, architects. General plan providing for 350 houses. From Architectural Record *43 (1918).*

106. Eclipse Park. Perspective and plans for eight-room house. Collection of the New-York Historical Society.

expected to make the lots more desirable than would have been the case with a static grid plan. William Pitkin Jr. was the landscape architect.

About thirty freestanding, single-family house designs were offered, all Colonial Revival in style, similar in materials, and ranging in size from four to eight rooms. The eight-room house would have been offered for about $2,850 (fig. 106). Eclipse Park was also expected to have shops, a movie theater, a library, and community meeting rooms in the square at the entrance to the park. Lawrence Veiller praised the scheme as marking "real progress in the housing of America's working people. While it cannot compare in beauty with the best developments of England, it gives promise of being one of the most artistic and attractive thus far evolved in this country."[9] The proposal, however, was only partly implemented. The company had expected about three hundred houses to be constructed, but only the northeastern section of the site was developed, and the community facilities were not constructed. Eighty of the houses built to the Post firm's designs are still extant.[10] Because the Eclipse Park project was presented in considerable detail in the professional journals, it was influential. James Otis Post helped to organize the United States Housing Bureau in 1918, and the U.S. Housing Corporation engaged the firm to design the town of Craddock, Virginia, its largest housing project.[11]

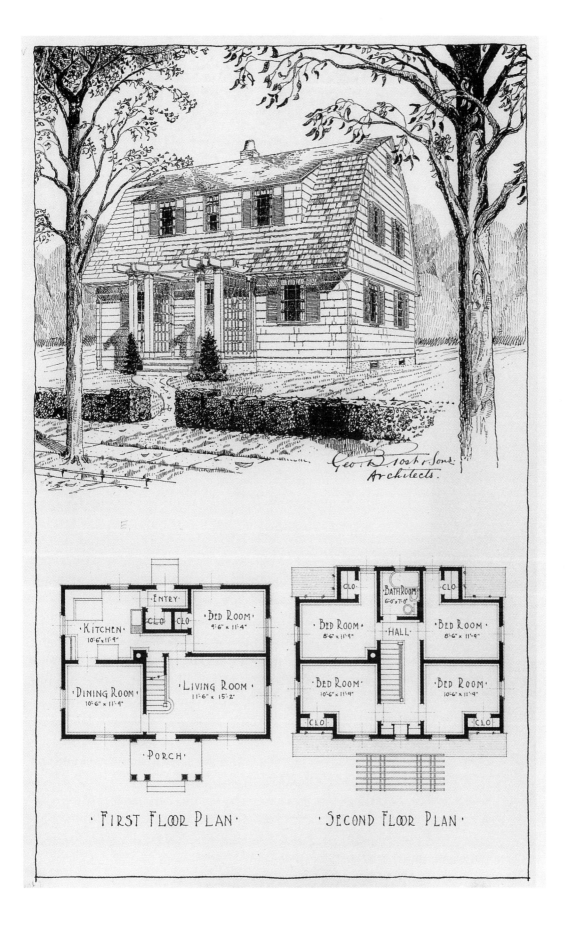

· FIRST FLOOR PLAN ·   · SECOND FLOOR PLAN ·

NOTES

The New-York Historical Society's
George B. Post Collection is hereafter
referred to as Post Collection.

CHAPTER 1

1. "Honor Memory of Late Local Man, One Hundreth Anniversary of the Birth of George B. Post, Architect," *Bernardsville News,* January 20, 1938, clippings file, Bernardsville Public Library; and W. Francklyn Paris, "George B. Post," *The Hall of American Artists* (New York: New York University, 1955), vol. 10, 35.

2. Marie Caroline de Trobriand Post, *The Post Family* (New York: Sterling Potter, 1905), 139. The author explains that Joel Post had acquired the Claremont property in 1820, and that the house and land along the Hudson River were purchased from his descendants by the city for the north end of Riverside Park. Grant's Tomb was erected on part of the property.

3. *Catalogue of the University* (1857–58), 19–20, New York University Archives; Montgomery Schuyler, "George Browne Post Obituary," *Architectural Record* 35 (January 1914): 94; and Paris, "George B. Post," 45.

4. Alan Burnham, ed., "The Richard Morris Hunt Papers, 1828–1895," comp. Catharine H. Hunt, 54–55, typescript, Avery Architectural and Fine Arts Library, Columbia University.

5. Paul R. Baker, *Richard Morris Hunt* (Cambridge, Mass.: MIT Press, 1980), 65–66, 100–105; Neil Levine, "The Romantic Idea of Architectural Legibility: Henri Labrouste and the Néo-Grec," in *The Architecture of the Ecole des Beaux-Arts,* ed. Arthur Drexler (New York: Museum of Modern Art, 1977), 331–33; and David Van Zanten, "Architectural Composition at the Ecole des Beaux-Arts from Charles Percier to Charles Garnier," *Architecture of the Ecole des Beaux-Arts,* 208.

6. Although initially accepted, Post's plans were found "to exceed the appropriation," newspaper article, July 24, 1888, Post Collection. John P. Leo's design was executed instead. According to Lisa B. Mausolf, "A Catalog of the Work of George B. Post, Architect" (master's thesis, Columbia University, 1983), 17–18 n.12, Leo had worked in Post's office from 1870 to 1886. Hereafter, unless otherwise indicated, all of Post's projects are listed with dates in Mausolf's "Catalog."

7. Joan H. King, "George Post: Recollections," *Bernardsville News,* January 14, 1982, clippings file, Bernardsville Public Library; and clippings scrapbook, Post Collection. Richard Upjohn designed the University Place Presbyterian Church (c.1845), which is no longer extant, and Minard Lafever designed Holy Trinity Church (1847), now the Church of St. Ann and the Holy Trinity.

8. According to Winston Weisman, "Post, George Browne" *Macmillan Encyclopedia of Architects,* ed. A. K. Placzek (New York: Free Press, 1982), vol. 3, 461, there is evidence in New York City Department of Buildings records that Post collaborated on a project with someone named Mead in the fall of 1867. Roxanne Kuter Williamson, *American Architects and the Mechanics of Fame* (Austin: University of Texas Press, 1991), 89 and 240–41 n.33, identifies Mead as Samuel Mead.

9. Sarah Bradford Landau and Carl W. Condit, *Rise of the New York Skyscraper, 1865–1913* (New Haven: Yale University Press, 1996), 67, 407 nn.10, 11; see 62–71 for a full

discussion of the building as completed with sources for information given here.

10. Quoted in Francisco Mujica, *History of the Skyscraper* (Paris: Archaeology and Architecture Press, 1929), 22.

11. I am indebted to Mosette Broderick for the address of Green's residence. On Green's relationship to New York University, see Theodore Francis Jones, ed., *New York University, 1832–1932* (New York: New York University Press, 1933), 72, 87, 88, 93, 101. On the Princeton buildings, see Princeton University, *The Princeton Book* (Boston: Houghton, Osgood and Co., 1879), 246; George R. Wallace, *Princeton Sketches* (New York: G. P. Putnam's Sons, 1893), 115; and T. J. Wertenbaker, *Princeton, 1746–1896* (Princeton University Press, 1946), 294–96.

12. *Princeton Book*, 246; and Sarah Bradford Landau, *Edward T. and William A. Potter, American Victorian Architects* (New York: Garland Publishing, 1979), 254–62. The questionnaire and Post's letters dated March 4 and 14 and April 25, 1871, are in the Princeton University Manuscripts Collection.

13. A. J. Bloor, "Annual Address," *Proceedings of the Tenth Annual Convention of the American Institute of Architects* (Boston: Franklin Press, Rand, Avery & Co., 1877), 25.

14. On bank buildings, see Lois Severini, *The Architecture of Finance: Early Wall Street* (Ann Arbor: UMI Research Press, 1983), 2–3 and passim; and Robert A. M. Stern, Gregory Gilmartin, and John Montague Massengale, *New York 1900: Metropolitan Architecture and Urbanism, 1890–1915* (New York: Rizzoli, 1983), 177. The Williamsburgh Savings Bank is described in "New Buildings in New York and Vicinity," *Manufacturer and Builder* 6 (February 1874): 33; see also Gale Harris, "Williamsburgh Savings Bank, First Floor Interior," New York City Landmarks Preservation Commission Designation Report, June 25, 1996.

15. Sarah Bradford Landau, *P. B. Wight: Architect, Contractor, and Critic, 1838–1925* (Chicago: Art Institute of Chicago, 1981), 28; and Harris, "Williamsburgh Savings Bank," 2–3 and 5. The building has been extended several times; since 1989, it has been owned by the Republic National Bank.

16. As quoted from Post's own description of his plans, dated December 30, 1871, in Henry-Russell Hitchcock and William Seale, *Temples of Democracy* (New York: Harcourt Brace Jovanovich, 1976), 160.

17. Basing her attribution on Post's letters to Porter in the Post Collection, Mausolf has identified Post's rendering as the Porter House: "Catalog," 6, 18 n.21, 34. The commission, but not the actual design, is also documented in Wight's records; see Landau, *P. B. Wight,* 78. Most of Post's residential buildings of the 1870s have been either demolished or altered, and the Post Collection contains few drawings or photographs of them.

18. The information given here is from Mendel Mesick Cohen Waite Architects, Development Plan: "Troy Savings Bank Music Hall," 1983, a thoroughly researched report that includes a full description of the Music Hall reprinted from the *Troy Daily Times,* April 15, 1875. The ironwork was supplied by the Architectural Ironworks, New York City, and the plasterwork was done by G. Garibaldi.

19. Bloor, "Annual Address," 25.

20. However, this elevator caused problems and was later replaced by a steam-powered model. See "The Western Union Telegraph Building," *Journal of the Telegraph* 8 (February 15, 1875): 49–51; see also Landau and Condit, *Rise of the New York Skyscraper,* 78–83, for a fuller discussion of the building.

21. Post's rendering is discussed as a probable preliminary study for the Western Union Building by Winston Weisman in "The Commercial Architecture of George B. Post," *Journal of the Society of Architectural Historians* 31 (October 1972): 182. It is correctly identified by Mausolf, "Catalog," 25. No longer extant, Peabody & Stearns's building is illustrated and described in *King's Handbook of Boston* (Cambridge, Mass.: Moses King, 1878), title page and 247–49; and documented in Wheaton Holden, "Robert Swain Peabody of Peabody and Stearns in Boston" (Ph.D. diss., Boston University, 1969), 59.

22. Mausolf, "Catalog," 44, 49; and Diana Balmori, "George B. Post: The Process of Design and the New American Architectural Office (1868–1913)," *Journal of the Society of Architectural Historians* 46 (December 1987): 350–51. On the quality of Chickering Hall's entertainment, see *King's Handbook of New York City*, 2nd ed. (Boston: Moses King, 1893), 68.

23. Robert Bruegmann, "Architecture of the Hospital, 1770–1870: Design and Technology" (Ph.D. diss., University of Pennsylvania, 1976), 116; summary of a paper presented by Bruegmann, "Two American Hospitals in 1876," *Journal of the Society of Architectural Historians* 35 (December 1976): 280–81; Mardges Bacon, *Ernest Flagg: Beaux-Arts Architect and Urban Reformer* (New York: Architectural History Foundation; Cambridge, Mass.: MIT Press, 1986), 94, 347 n.71; and Eric Larrabee, *The Benevolent and Necessary Institution: The New York Hospital,*

1771–1971 (Garden City: Doubleday & Company, 1971), 234–45. The building was described and illustrated in *The Daily Graphic: New York* 13 (March 17, 1877): 115–16; and *Harper's Weekly* 21 (April 7, 1877): 267, 272.

24. Bloor, "Annual Address," 23.

25. *New York Hospital, Report of the Building Committee together with an Address delivered on the Occasion of the Inauguration of the New Building* (New York: L. W. Lawrence, Stationer, 1877), 25; see also 30–32.

26. James Taylor, "The History of Terra Cotta in New York City," *Architectural Record* 2 (October–December 1892): 144.

27. Susan Tunick, *Terra-Cotta Skyline: New York's Architectural Ornament* (New York: Princeton Architectural Press, 1997), 18. Sources conflict on the address of the house, but Post's job record book for 1870–90 (Post Collection) and city directories from the late 1870s and 1880s give it as 15 East 36th Street. The directories also list Braem's occupations. His name is frequently spelled there as "Henri."

28. According to the minutes of the Long Island Historical Society for January 8, 1881, the committee made its decision on September 26, 1878. A copy of the competition instructions is held with the Upjohn Papers (Box 6) in the New York Public Library; the Brooklyn Historical Society has another copy and also holds several of the competition designs as well as the minutes.

29. Beth Sullebarger, "The Long Island Historical Society: A Building History" (July 1984), 18, and also 13, where it is stated that Post himself contributed five hundred dollars to the building fund and that his third scheme was selected. Sullebarger's unpublished paper is included as Appendix II in Jan Hird Pokorny, Architects and Planners, "The Brooklyn Historical Society: Historic Structure Report" (1993), vol. 2. Pokorny is the architect for the renovation and restoration of the building, a project planned for 1998–99; his firm's three-volume report provides a thoroughly documented account. Appendix III of the report is Lori Zabar's paper, "The Long Island Historical Society Building" (n.d.); and Appendix IV is Ruth Pasquine's paper, "George Post's Long Island Historical Society: Evolution and Style, 1877–1880" (February 15, 1986).

30. "Design for an Art-Institute," *Appletons' Journal of Popular Culture* 2 (November 27, 1869): 460. This article is filed with other clippings in the Post Collection; the "Inspirational Designs" are also held in the Post Collection.

31. Pokorny, "Brooklyn Historical Society," vol. 1, 11–13.

32. *American Architect and Building News* 2 (February 3, 1877): 36. Another unidentified rendering in the Post Collection shows a church similar to this one, also with a heavy crossing tower like Trinity's, but High Victorian Gothic in style. That drawing is signed by Post and dated 1877, hence my dating of the rendering illustrated here. Perhaps Post offered his prospective client a choice of styles.

33. Post's design was published in *Plumber and Sanitary Engineer* 2 (April 1879): 124; see also James Ford, *Slums and Housing* (Cambridge, Mass.: Harvard University Press, 1936), vol. 1, 185, and vol. 2, 872; and Richard Plunz, *A History of Housing in New York City* (New York: Columbia University Press, 1990), 18–20. Post's tenements include five at 1301–1309 Third Avenue with commercial space on the ground floor and, around the corner, six of an original matching set of ten, at 202–208 and 216–218 East 75th Street. These modest, brick-fronted buildings, each three windows wide like rowhouses, were financed by Thomas Smith, built in 1870–71, and designed to house one family per floor.

CHAPTER 2

1. According to Jonathan P. Harding, curator at the Century Association, Post was nominated for membership by his partner Charles D. Gambrill and became a member in 1863.

2. Mosette Glaser Broderick and William C. Shopsin, *The Villard Houses* (New York: Viking Press, 1980), 141 n.45 and 46–47; and Diana Balmori, "George B. Post: The Process of Design and the New American Architectural Office (1868–1913)," *Journal of the Society of Architectural Historians* 46 (December 1987): 34–45. See also John Foreman and Robbe Pierce Stimson, *The Vanderbilts and the Gilded Age: Architectural Aspirations, 1879–1901* (New York: St. Martin's Press, 1991), chap. 3. W. H. Vanderbilt's twin residences were designed by John B. Snook and the Herter Brothers and built at the same time as Post's and Hunt's chateaus.

3. The Fisk project is illustrated and discussed in Mosette Broderick, "Fifth Avenue," in *The Grand American Avenue, 1850–1920,* ed. J. Cigliano and S. B. Landau (San Francisco: Pomegranate Artbooks, 1994), 18. See also Montgomery Schuyler, "Recent Buildings in New York—V: The Vanderbilt Houses," *American Architect and Building News* 9 (May 21, 1881): 243–44 and illustrations; and Schuyler, "The Vanderbilt Houses," in *American Architecture and Other Writings,* ed. William Jordy and Ralph Coe (Cambridge, Mass.: Harvard University Press, 1961), vol. 2, 488–501.

4. As quoted in Mardges Bacon, *Ernest Flagg: Beaux-Arts Architect and Urban Reformer* (New York: Architectural History Foundation; Cambridge, Mass.: MIT Press, 1986), 15; see also 313 nn.72, 73.

5. Alan Burnham, ed., "The Richard Morris Hunt Papers, 1828–1895," comp. Catharine H. Hunt, 259, typescript, Avery Architectural and Fine Arts Library, Columbia University.

6. Russell Sturgis, "The Works of George B. Post," *Great American Architects Series,* no. 4, *Architectural Record* (June 1898): 56.

7. Sturgis, "Works," 56–83; Dianne H. Pilgrim, "Decorative Art: The Domestic Environment," *The American Renaissance, 1876–1917* (New York: Brooklyn Museum, 1979), 120–21; *In Pursuit of Beauty: Americans and the Aesthetic Movement* (New York: Metropolitan Museum of Art, 1986), passim; and the clippings scrapbook, Post Collection. The monumental Saint-Gaudens entrance hall mantelpiece was donated to the Metropolitan Museum; Saint-Gaudens's Ceres panel, originally in the dining room, is at the Saint-Gaudens National Historic Site; and his Acteon panel, also from the dining room, is in the J. B. Speed Art Museum in Louisville, Kentucky. On the relocation of the interior decoration during the 1892–94 enlargement as well as other survivals, see James L. Yarnall, "Souvenirs of Splendor: John La Farge and the Patronage of Cornelius Vanderbilt II," *American Art Journal* 26 (1994): 66–105.

8. William H. Jordy and Christopher P. Monkhouse, *Buildings on Paper: Rhode Island Architectural Drawings, 1825–1945* (Providence: Brown University, 1982), 20–21, 140–41. A photograph of the Baldwin house was published in *L'Architecture Américaine,* pt. 3 (Paris, 1886).

9. Montgomery Schuyler, "Concerning Queen Anne," in Jordy and Coe, *American Architecture,* vol. 2, 584; and Sturgis, "Works," 34–35. See also "The Post Building," *Real Estate Record and Builders Guide* 30 (November 11–18, 1882): 72–73; Winston Weisman, "The Commercial Architecture of George B. Post," *Journal of the Society of Architectural Historians* 31 (October 1972): 186; and Sarah Bradford Landau and Carl W. Condit, *Rise of the New York Skyscraper, 1865–1913* (New Haven: Yale University Press, 1996), 113–14.

10. The artist is not identified, but the grille was made by J. B. & J. M. Cornell of New York City: *American Architect and Building News* 12 (October 14, 1882): 182 and illustration. On the Mills Building, see Landau and Condit, *Rise of the New York Skyscraper,* 114–15.

11. "The New York Produce Exchange Competition," *American Architect and Building News* 9 (March 12, 1881): 123. This discussion of the Produce Exchange is based on Landau and Condit, *Rise of the New York Skyscraper,* 116–25 and related notes.

12. New York Produce Exchange, *Origin, Growth, and Usefulness of the New York Produce Exchange* (New York: Historical Publishing, 1884), 57.

13. Susan Tunick, *Terra-Cotta Skyline: New York's Architectural Ornament* (New York: Princeton Architectural Press, 1997), 19–20. Kemeys also sculpted the terra-cotta animal heads on the stable Post designed for the Cornelius Vanderbilt mansion: "Notes and Clippings," *American Architect and Building News* 8 (November 6, 1880): 225.

14. The building's sophisticated plumbing system is described in Landau and Condit, *Rise of the New York Skyscraper,* 128–31.

15. Quotation from "The Mortimer Building," *Real Estate Record and Builders Guide* 34 (December 13, 1884): 1247.

16. Weisman, "Commercial Architecture," 191.

17. New building docket 894-1872, New York City Building Records Collection, Municipal Archives, New York City. See also Lisa B. Mausolf, "A Catalog of the Work of George B. Post, Architect" (master's thesis, Columbia University, 1983), 22 n.58, 25, 29, and 35. The narrow-fronted but very deep Black Building has the unusual feature of being L-shaped, with a nearly one-hundred-foot-long wing extending into the block.

18. New York City Landmarks Preservation Commission, "South Street Seaport Historic District Designation Report," May 10, 1977, 9.

19. Burnham, "Richard Morris Hunt Papers," 172; and Roscoe Carlyle Buley, *The Equitable Life Assurance Society of the United States, 1859–1964* (New York: Appleton-Century Crofts, 1967), vol. 1, 312. Raht became the architect of Equitable's foreign buildings.

20. Quotations from newspaper clippings in the Post Collection. See also Landau and Condit, *Rise of the New York Skyscraper,* 71–75.

21. *New York Herald,* June 12, 1888. Edward B. Wesley, a founder of the New York Times, had been a member of the building committee of the Western Union Building and may have helped Post secure this commission; see Balmori, "George B. Post," 355. In the obituary "Dean of Speculators, Edward B. Wesley, Dies," *New York Times,* October 4, 1906, Wesley was also credited with being a founder and trustee of the Union Trust Company, for which Post would design the Union Trust Building (1889–90).

22. Balmori, "George B. Post," 351; and Landau and Condit, *Rise of the New York Skyscraper,* 149–55.

23. Montgomery Schuyler, "The 'Sky-scraper' Up To Date," *Architectural Record* 8 (January–

March 1899): 233.

24. Landau and Condit, *Rise of the New York Skyscraper,* 194–97, 173.

25. *Mail and Express,* March 20, 1889, clipping, Post Collection.

26. Discussion here based on Landau and Condit, *Rise of the New York Skyscraper,* 197–201. Bitter may not have been responsible for all of the figural sculpture, according to James M. Dennis, *Karl Bitter, Architectural Sculptor 1867–1915* (Madison: University of Wisconsin Press, 1967), 37–38; see also 19–20.

27. Burnham, "Richard Morris Hunt Papers," 184.

28. Burnham, "Richard Morris Hunt Papers," 184.

29. Sturgis, "Works," 83; see also 83–93. For a detailed and thoroughly documented account of this house, see Isabelle Hyman, "The Huntington Mansion in New York: Economics of Architecture and Decoration in the 1890s," *Syracuse University Library Associates Courier* 25 (fall 1990): 3–29.

CHAPTER 3

1. However he may have left because he was dissatisfied with the Horgan & Slattery firm's control of the department; see the clippings scrapbook, Post Collection. According to Morrison H. Heckscher, *The Metropolitan Museum of Art: An Architectural History* (New York: Metropolitan Museum of Art, 1995), 34, Post was appointed consulting architect for the museum in 1896 because of the "relative inexperience" of Hunt's son, Richard Howland Hunt, who took over the project after his father's death in 1895.

2. Diana Balmori, "George B. Post: The Process of Design and the New American Architectural Office (1868–1913)," *Journal of the Society of Architectural Historians* 46 (December 1987): 351.

3. Winston Weisman, "The Commercial Architecture of George B. Post," *Journal of the Society of Architectural Historians* 31 (October 1972): 194; see also the clippings scrapbook, Post Collection.

4. Clipping dated April 1890, Post Collection.

5. Clipping dated April 1890, Post Collection.

6. Inspired by Bruce Price's 1890 project for the Sun Building in New York and by the Campanile of San Marco in Venice, Post had proposed a similar tower for the Equitable Building in about 1897. These are discussed and illustrated in Weisman, "Commercial Architecture," 197–98. The new fountain is described in *Newark Sunday Call,* March 9, 1902, the clippings scrapbook, Post Collection. It was donated to the Newark Museum when the building was demolished and is now displayed in the museum's garden court.

7. James Otis Post, "Recent and Current Work

of George B. Post & Sons," *New York Architect* 3 (June 1909): 8–10; "The Prudential Group, Newark, N.J.: George B. Post & Sons, Architects," *New York Architect* 5 (October 1911): 193–94; *The Prudential Insurance Company of America . . . Home Office, Newark, New Jersey* (Newark: Prudential Co., 1917), unpaged; Earl Chapin May and Will Oursler, *A Story of Human Security: The Prudential* (Garden City, N.Y.: Doubleday, 1950), 112–13 and 174; William H. A. Carr, *From Three Cents A Week . . . The Story of the Prudential Insurance Company of America* (Englewood Cliffs, N.J.: Prentice-Hall, 1975), 62 and 201–3; and newspaper articles in the collection of the Newark Public Library. Post's Newark commissions also included buildings for the Callender Factory Company (1884) in East Newark, the Howard Savings Bank (1898–99), Mutual Benefit Life Insurance (1899), Public Service Corporation (1911–13), and the YMCA (1912–13).

8. Russell Sturgis, "The Works of George B. Post," *Great American Architects Series,* no. 4, *Architectural Record* (June 1898): 24. See also National Audubon Society fact sheet; and National Audubon Society and Croxton Collaborative Architects, *Audubon House: Building the Environmentally Responsible, Energy-Efficient Office* (New York: John Wiley & Sons, 1994). In 1911–12, Post altered the building, possibly adding the penthouse.

9. Alan Burnham, ed., "The Richard Morris Hunt Papers, 1828–1895," comp. Catharine H. Hunt, 241, typescript, Avery Architectural and Fine Arts Library, Columbia University.

10. Quotation (often repeated) from William E. Cameron, *The World's Fair, Being a Pictorial History of the Columbian Exposition* (Waterville, Maine: Sawyer Publishing Co., 1893), 371. Chapter 21 of this book describes the building and its exhibits in detail.

11. "World's Columbian Exposition, Erection of the Manufactures Building," *Engineering News,* supplement (July 28, 1892): 74.

12. "Dinner to George B. Post," *New York Evening Post,* December 16, 1897. See also Pauline King, *American Mural Painting: A Study of the Important Decorations by Distinguished Artists in the United States* (Boston: Noyes, Platt & Company, 1902), 263–64. According to James M. Dennis, *Karl Bitter, Architectural Sculptor 1867–1915* (Madison: University of Wisconsin Press, 1967), 270 n.7, Bitter designed only one relief for Post's building. Cameron, *World's Fair,* 373, writes that all of them were Bitter's.

13. Donald Hoffmann, "Clear Span Rivalry: The World's Fairs of 1889–1893," *Journal of the Society of Architectural Historians* 29 (March 1970): 48–50; Titus M. Karlowitz, "Notes on

the Columbian Exposition's Manufactures and Liberal Arts Building," *Journal of the Society of Architectural Historians* 33 (October 1974): 214–18; and John W. Stamper, "The Galerie des Machines of the 1889 Paris World's Fair," *Technology and Culture* 30 (April 1989): 351.

14. "Havemeyer Building," *Real Estate Record and Builders Guide* 51 (January 28, 1893): 133.

15. Sarah Bradford Landau and Carl W. Condit, *Rise of the New York Skyscraper, 1865–1913* (New Haven: Yale University Press, 1996), 205–8.

16. The clippings scrapbook, Post Collection; Walter C. Kidney, *Pittsburgh's Landmark Architecture: The Historic Buildings of Pittsburgh and Allegheny County* (Pittsburgh History & Landmarks Foundation, 1985), 84 and 236–37; and Franklin Toker, *Pittsburgh: An Urban Portrait* (University Park: Pennsylvania University Press, 1986), 44.

17. Sturgis, "Works," 46–47, 49–52; and Dennis, *Karl Bitter,* 123. Blashfield's murals were exhibited in New York before they were installed; see the clippings scrapbook, Post Collection.

18. Clippings in the collection of the Pittsburgh History & Landmarks Foundation; and Kidney, *Pittsburgh's Landmark Architecture,* 509.

19. Sturgis, "Works," 47.

20. See Michael Cheilik and David Gillison's pamphlet, *Public Buildings in the Bronx* (New York: Herbert H. Lehman College, City University of New York, 1980?); and "New Interior for Abandoned Relic," *Architectural and Engineering News* 10 (September 1968): 32–33.

21. The ground-floor front on Broadway has been altered, but the rear lobby is intact. At first this was called the Meyer-Jonasson building; see the clippings scrapbook, Post Collection.

22. Quotations from minutes of A. J. Bloor, secretary, in "New York Chapter, A.I.A.—High Building Limit," *American Architect* 52 (May 30, 1896): 86–87. For more on efforts to restrict building heights, see Landau and Condit, *Rise of the New York Skyscraper,* 188–89 and passim.

23. "The Most Modern Instance," *Real Estate Record and Builders Guide* 59 (June 5, 1897): 962.

24. Montgomery Schuyler, "The 'Sky-scraper' Up To Date," *Architectural Record* 8 (January–March 1899): 236; and Weisman, "Commercial Architecture," 197. See the discussion of the St. Paul Building in Landau and Condit, *Rise of the New York Skyscraper,* 238–42.

25. When the St. Paul Building was demolished in 1958 the atlantes were given to the city of Indianapolis, which installed them in Holiday Park; see Dennis, *Karl Bitter,* 65, and also 64–68.

26. *Proceedings of the Thirtieth Annual Convention of the American Institute of Architects* (Providence: E. A. Johnson & Co., Printers, 1896), 10.

27. *Proceedings of the Thirty-First Annual Convention* (1897), 10 and 12.

28. American Institute of Architects minutes for October 14, 1895, American Institute of Architects Library and Archives, Washington, D.C.; *Proceedings of the Thirty-First Annual Convention* (1897), 11–12; *Proceedings of the Thirty-Second Annual Convention* (1898), 10–11; Paul R. Baker, *Richard Morris Hunt* (Cambridge, Mass.: MIT Press, 1980), 436–38; and Sarah Bradford Landau, "Coming to Terms: Architecture Competitions in America and the Emerging Profession, 1789–1922," in *The Experimental Tradition,* ed. Hélène Lipstadt (New York: Princeton Architectural Press, 1989), 65.

29. Newspaper and journal articles of 1900–1901, the clippings scrapbook, Post Collection.

30. "Architect George B. Post's Project for a Glorified Manhattan Island," *New York World,* January 8, 1899, clipping in Post Collection; "Correspondence," *American Architect and Building News* 2 (July 28, 1877): 242; Henry F. Hornbostel, "Proposed Brooklyn Bridge Terminal and City Offices," *Architects' and Builders' Magazine* 4 (August 1903): 483–89; Gregory F. Gilmartin, *Shaping the City: New York and the Municipal Art Society* (New York: Clarkson N. Potter, 1995), 78–79; and Landau and Condit, *Rise of the New York Skyscraper,* 366–67.

31. The first house in the area designed by Post seems to have been the William Z. Larned House (1884) at 44 Blackburn Road in Summit, New Jersey, now the Oak Knoll School of the Holy Child. One of the best sources of information on Bernardsville was written by one of Post's sons, Allison Wright Post, *Recollections of Bernardsville, New Jersey, 1871–1941* (New York: J. J. Little & Ives, 1941). See also Bernardsville History Book Committee, *Among the Blue Hills . . . Bernardsville . . . A History* (Newark, N.J.: Johnston Letter Co., 1991), esp. chapters 5 and 6; and clippings, Bernardsville Public Library and Post Collection. Stronghold was enlarged by Post in 1904, and by his successor firm in 1916–17 for John Dryden's son, Forrest F. Dryden, who succeeded his father as president of Prudential in 1912.

32. "William Post, 74: Noted Architect," *New York Times,* July 9, 1940, 21; see also Marie Caroline de Trobriand Post, *The Post Family* (New York: Sterling Potter, 1905), 178. William Post designed the Arthur C. Train house at 113 East 73rd Street in New York (1906–8). The Train house was not demolished as stated in Lisa B. Mausolf, "A Catalog of the Work of George B. Post, Architect"

(master's thesis, Columbia University, 1983), 42, but was rebuilt and refronted as an addition to the Buckley School in 1962; see Robert A. M. Stern, Thomas Mellins, and David Fishman, *New York 1960: Architecture and Urbanism between the Second World War and the Bicentennial* (New York: The Monacelli Press, 1995), 838, 1098.

33. Quotations and information from "Immense Museum Designed for New York," *New York Press,* November 12, 1899, the clippings scrapbook, Post Collection.

CHAPTER 4

1. Directory of NYSE Members, New York Stock Exchange Archives. George B. Post Jr. was a founder c.1889 of the New York brokerage firm Post & Flagg.

2. Minutes of the Committee on Plan and Scope, New York Stock Exchange, December 18, 1898, to November 24, 1899; and Minutes of the Governing Committee, New York Stock Exchange, 1900–1901, New York Stock Exchange Archives. See also Deborah S. Gardner, *Marketplace: A Brief History of the New York Stock Exchange* (New York Stock Exchange, 1982), unpaged; James E. Buck, ed., *The New York Stock Exchange: The First 200 Years* (Essex, Conn.: Greenwich Publishing Group, 1992), 69, 90, 94; and Robert A. M. Stern, Gregory Gilmartin, and John Montague Massengale, *New York 1900: Metropolitan Architecture and Urbanism, 1890–1915* (New York: Rizzoli, 1983), 187–89. According to Lisa B. Mausolf, "A Catalog of the Work of George B. Post, Architect" (master's thesis, Columbia University, 1983), 27, Post had competed unsuccessfully in 1884 for the job of altering and enlarging the old building, and had also been involved in plans for altering it a year or so later.

3. Russell Sturgis, "Facade of the New York Stock Exchange," *Architectural Record* 16 (November 1904): 474. See also Lewis I. Sharp, *John Quincy Adams Ward, Dean of American Sculpture* (Newark, N.J.: University of Delaware Press, 1985), 89 and 263–64. Having deteriorated due to their weight and flaws in the marble, the pedimental sculptures were replaced with lead-covered copper replicas in 1936.

4. "The Story of the New Stock Exchange," *Mail and Express,* supplement, April 22, 1903, 3, New York Stock Exchange Archives. This source explains that it took longer than expected to demolish the old building because it required blasting that had to be carefully handled, since the site was

surrounded by buildings (17–18). For a detailed account of how the building was designed and the changes that Post had to make in his original plan for the trading floor, see Percy C. Stuart, "The New York Stock Exchange," *Architectural Record* 11 (July 1901): 525–55.

5. Montgomery Schuyler, "The New Stock Exchange," *Architectural Record* 12 (September 1902): 413–14.

6. "Story of the New Stock Exchange," 7.

7. Bernard A. Nagengast, "Alfred Wolff—HVAC Pioneer," *ASHRAE Journal* 32 (January 1990): S80; and Cecil D. Elliott, *Technics and Architecture: The Development of Materials and Systems for Buildings* (Cambridge, Mass.: MIT Press, 1992), 316–17. See also New York Stock Exchange Building Committee transcripts, 1901–3, New York Stock Exchange Archives. In 1920–22 a compatible twenty-three-story addition was built to the plans of Trowbridge & Livingston, a firm whose founders had started out in Post's office. At that time, the trading floor was expanded, and other changes have been made since then as the volume of trading and the need for electronic equipment have increased.

8. Répertoire d'architecture traditionnelle sur le territoire de la Communauté urbaine de Montréal, *Architecture Commerciale I. Les Banques* (Montreal: Service de la planification du territoire, 1980), 124–25; and Francois Remillard and Brian Merrett, *L'Architecture de Montréal: Guide des styles et des bâtiments* (Montreal: Meridien, 1990), 116. According to "Building in Canada in 1894," *Canadian Architect and Builder* 8 (January 1895): 8, Post took over from a Montreal firm as architect on the Montreal Street Railway Company Building about 1895.

9. Russell Sturgis, "The Works of George B. Post," *Great American Architects Series,* no. 4, *Architectural Record* (June 1898): 102.

10. Arthur Ebbs Willauer, "The College of the City of New York," *American Architect and Building News* 93, pt. 1 (May 13, 1908): 156; and "Office Force Record Book," Post Collection, where Willauer is listed as working in the office from December 15, 1898, to October 7, 1901. On the various problems, see S. Willis Rudy, *The College of the City of New York: A History, 1847–1947* (New York: City College Press, 1949), 220–22 and 257–58.

11. This plan, which is in the Post Collection, was exhibited in 1899; see A. D. F. Hamlin and F. S. Lamb, "The New York Architectural League Exhibition," *Architectural Review* 6 (March 1899): 44.

12. Post is quoted in Arthur Ebbs Willauer, "The College of the City of New York," *American Architect and Building News* 93, pt. 2 (May 20,

1908): 167. Many of Post's preliminary renderings were published in newspapers and professional journals, for example, "College of the City of New York," *Architecture* 7 (March 15, 1903): 28–32; "The City College of New York," *Architectural Review* 12 (December 1905): 305–12; and "City College's New Home," *New-York Tribune Illustrated Supplement,* March 8, 1908, clipping in Post Collection.

13. On the Post campus, see also Stern et al., *New York 1900,* 108–9; and Paul David Pearson, *The City College of New York: 150 Years of Academic Architecture* (New York: City College of the City University of New York, 1997), 5–26. Pearson discusses and illustrates an unexecuted design of 1909 by Post for a library to have been sited at the corner of West 138th Street and Amsterdam Avenue (23–24).

14. Willauer, "College of the City of New York," pt. 1, 158. The stone is often said to have come from the excavations for the subway system under construction at the time, but this may be a confusion over the term "subway," which was also used in contemporary sources to describe the underground passageway connecting Post's buildings; see James E. Dibble, "City College, City University of New York, North Campus," New York City Landmarks Preservation Commission designation report, 1981, 24 n.14.

15. Montgomery Schuyler, "The College of the City of New York," *Architectural Record* 21 (March 1907): 176; and Schuyler, "Architecture of American Colleges IV: New York City Colleges," *Architectural Record* 27 (June 1910): 463–64. Schuyler had also disliked the color scheme and combination of materials Post used for the Cornelius Vanderbilt mansion. See Montgomery Schuyler, "Recent Buildings in New York— V: The Vanderbilt Houses," *American Architect and Building News* 9 (May 21, 1881): 244.

16. Willauer, "College of the City of New York," pt. 2, 164; Dibble, "City College," with illustrations giving Smith's name as the artist, 10–11; *Architecture* 12 (November 15, 1905): 172–73, where twenty unsigned drawings of grotesques are illustrated; and Pearson, *City College,* 22. Pearson names G. Grandellis as the modeler. Several of Post's City College buildings have been restored recently.

17. From Post's letter to Lew Porter of January 6, 1908, Wisconsin Capitol Commission records, as quoted in Joyce Rae Inman, "Documentation of George B. Post's Design for the Senate Chamber of the Wisconsin State Capitol" (master's thesis, University of Wisconsin—Madison, 1995), 102.

18. Illustrations in *Architecture* 10 (December 15,

1904): 194–96. Two of Post's competition drawings were exhibited in 1905: *Catalogue of the Twentieth Annual Exhibition of the Architectural League of New York* (1905), exhibits 469 and 471.

19. The estate has remained in the Post family and includes Post's shingled stable–coach house built in 1904.

20. According to "William Post, 74: Noted Architect," *New York Times,* July 9, 1940, 21; "he himself drew the general plan for the buildings of City College." It should be noted, however, that George Post made the watercolor renderings for the buildings. Also, "Post, James Otis," *National Cyclopedia of American Biography,* vol. 42 (New York: James T. White & Co., 1958), 108–9.

21. "Keppel, Frederick," *National Cyclopedia of American Biography,* vol. 22 (New York: James T. White & Co., 1932), 386. See also Christopher Gray, "Streetscapes: Reader's Questions," *New York Times,* December 2, 1990.

22. Office of the University Historian, *The George Washington University, 1821–1966* (Washington, D.C.: George Washington University, 1966), 18; see also newspaper articles of January 28, 1906, in the clippings scrapbook, Post Collection.

23. Cleveland Landmarks Commission, "National Register of Historic Places Inventory— Nomination Form, November 26, 1973," unpaged.

24. "National Register Nomination Form"; James M. Dennis, *Karl Bitter, Architectural Sculptor 1867–1915* (Madison: University of Wisconsin Press, 1967), 120–22; and "An Elegant New Bank Building," *Ohio Architect and Builder,* January 1908, 36–39, collection of the Cleveland Landmarks Commission.

25. John J. Grabowski and Walter C. Leedy Jr., *The Terminal Tower, Tower City Center: A Historical Perspective* (Cleveland: Western Reserve Historical Society, 1990), 25. According to clippings in the collection of the Cleveland Landmarks Commission, Post's successor firm was first selected to design the Hotel Cleveland in 1916, but the commission went to Graham, Burnham & Co. instead; the Cleveland Trust Branch at East 55th Street and Woodland Avenue (demolished) was built to the design of Alfred G. Hall, not that of Post's firm; and the Post firm's Cleveland Trust Perry Street Branch (c.1917) seems to have been at East 22nd Street rather than East 29th Street as listed by Mausolf, "Catalog," 56.

26. From Thomas Spees Carrington, *Tuberculosis Hospital and Sanatorium Construction* (New York: W. T. Comstock, 1911), as cited in New Jersey Department of Human Services, "Historic American Buildings Survey: New

Jersey State Tuberculosis Sanatorium," January 1997, 7.

27. Quotations from James Otis Post and S. S. Goldwater, "The New Samaritan Hospital, Troy, N.Y.," reprinted from *Modern Hospital* 4 (January 1915): 1, Post Collection.

28. Post and Goldwater, "New Samaritan Hospital," 2–10; Leora E. Belknap, R.N., *The Story of Samaritan: A History of the Hospital, School of Nursing, and the Eddy Memorial Foundation* (Troy, N.Y.: Samaritan Hospital Foundation, 1990), chaps. 4 and 5; and William S. Post and S. S. Goldwater, "The New Mount Sinai Hospital of Cleveland," reprinted from *Modern Hospital* 6 (February 1916), Post Collection. Other hospitals and hospital additions designed by the Post firm were the Stamford (Conn.) Hospital (1911–13; additions of c.1925 and 1930 also by the Post firm); an addition to Vassar Brothers Hospital, Poughkeepsie, N.Y. (c.1912); the Massena (N.Y.) Municipal Hospital (c.1943); and St. Mary's Hospital for Children in Bayside, Queens, N.Y. (1949–51).

29. "The National Arts Club Studio Building, East 19th St., New York, N.Y.," *American Architect and Building News* 90 (November 17, 1906): 159 and plates. On the phenomenon of duplex and studio apartments, see Stern et al., *New York 1900,* which includes a discussion of the National Arts Club Studio Building, 298.

30. "George Browne Post, N.A., LL.D," *Nelson's Biographical Cyclopedia of New Jersey* (New York: Eastern Historical Publishing Society, 1913), vol. 2, 737–39; T. F. Hamlin, "Post, George Browne," *Dictionary of American Biography,* vol. 15 (New York: Charles Scribner's Sons, 1943), 115–16; and *Proceedings of the Forty-Fourth Annual Convention of the American Institute of Architects* (Washington, D.C.: Gibson Bros., Printers and Publishers, 1911), 148–49.

31. As quoted in Henry-Russell Hitchcock and William Seale, *Temples of Democracy* (New York: Harcourt Brace Jovanovich, 1976), 196.

32. Inman, "Documentation," 112. Also, State of Wisconsin Department of Administration, Division of Facilities Development; Kahler Slater Architects, Inc.; and Joyce Inman, Historic Interiors, *Historic Structure Report,* bk. 5 (1997), I-2, I-3. Inman's thesis and this report provide a detailed history of the building based on Wisconsin Capitol Commission records in the collection of the Wisconsin State Historical Society. Led by Charles J. Quagliana, AIA, State Capitol Project Manager and Preservation Architect, restoration and rehabilitation of the capitol building has been underway since 1988.

33. State of Wisconsin et al., *Historic Structure Report,* bk. 5, I-5.

34. George B. Post & Sons to Wisconsin State Capitol Commission, June 12, 1906, Box 20 (folder 16), Wisconsin Capitol Commission records.

35. On the influence of the Rhode Island Capitol, and also Cass Gilbert's Minnesota Capitol (1896–1903), see Hitchcock and Seale, *Temples of Democracy,* 262; and Inman, "Documentation," 119–20.

36. William S. Post was there only five times, but between 1906 and 1917, James Otis Post came twenty-three times; see Inman, "Documentation," 58, and also 114–16 on the structure and plan of the building.

37. Dennis, *Karl Bitter,* 132–47; State of Wisconsin et al., *Historic Structure Report,* bk. 5, 3-32 to 3-34. Also, Michael A. Mikkelsen, "The New Wisconsin State Capitol," *Architectural Record* 42 (September 1917): 194–233.

38. Letter of December 14, 1913, in Box 22 (folder 4), Wisconsin Capitol Commission records. Houston's telegram is also in Box 22 (folder 4).

39. Assisted by the Reverend Francisco Pescaturo, pastor of the First Italian Church of Newark, Basking Ridge Church members had for some time been holding Sunday School classes for the Italians in private homes. Post also designed the church parsonage; from Bernardsville History Book Committee, *Among the Blue Hills . . . Bernardsville . . . A History* (Newark, N.J.: Johnston Letter Co., 1991), 64–65 and 101–2.

40. "Dinner to George B. Post," *New York Evening Post,* December 16, 1897. Four hundred men were said to have attended the dinner, which was held in the Vanderbilt Gallery of the Art Students' League Building, then known as the American Fine-Arts Society Building.

41. "Post, George Browne," *National Cyclopedia of American Biography,* vol. 15 (1916), 252.

Post-Script

1. From his letter of December 27, 1907, to Capitol Commission member O. H. Ingram, and as quoted in Joyce Rae Inman, "Documentation of George B. Post's Design for the Senate Chamber of the Wisconsin State Capitol" (master's thesis, University of Wisconsin—Madison, 1995), 108.

2. "Post, James Otis," *National Cyclopedia of American Biography,* vol. 42 (New York: James T. White & Co., 1958), 108. See also "George B. Post & Sons, Architects," unpublished pamphlet (c.1995) with chronology of the successor firm compiled by Dorothy S. Post, daughter of Edward Everett Post. Although

the entire office was moved to Long Island in 1972, the successor firm was listed at 101 Park Avenue in New York City directories until 1981.

3. Floyd Miller, *America's Extraordinary Hotelman Statler* (New York: Statler Foundation, 1968), 132. Eisenwein & Johnson designed the 1908 Buffalo Statler Hotel: "Hotel Statler in Buffalo, N.Y.," *Architectural Review* 2 (April 1913): 104.

4. W. Sydney Wagner, "The Statler Idea in Hotel Planning and Equipment," *Architectural Forum* 27 (November 1917): 118. The Post firm's project architect for the Cleveland, Detroit, and St. Louis Statler hotels was W. Sydney Wagner, and this is the first of four articles he wrote for *Architectural Forum* on the subject. The others are in the December 1917 and January and February 1918 issues. Also, Wagner, "The Hotel Statler in Detroit," *Architectural Record* 37 (April 1915): 320–39.

5. *Cleveland Plain Dealer,* October 20, 1912. In 1954 the Statler chain was purchased by Conrad Hilton.

6. J. Otis Post, "Efficient Planning for Economical Operation," *Architectural Forum* 51 (December 1929): 667; and Robert A. M. Stern, Gregory Gilmartin, and Thomas Mellins, *New York 1930: Architecture and Urbanism Between the Two World Wars* (New York: Rizzoli, 1987), 203, 779 n.13.

7. "Hearst, William Randolph," *National Cyclopedia of American Biography,* vol. 39 (1954), 9; Mary Jean Madigan, "Gotham Remembered," *Restaurant/Hotel Design International* 11 (November 1989): 79; W. Parker Chase, *New York The Wonder City,* 1932 (c.1931; reprint, New York: New York Bound, 1983), 136; Stern et al., *New York 1930,* 239, 621; and Janet Adams, "Hearst Magazine Building," New York City Landmarks Preservation Commission designation report, February 16, 1988, 8–9.

8. Ralph F. Warner of George B. Post & Sons, "A Wage Earners' Community Development at Beloit, Wisconsin," *American Architect and Building News* 113 (May 22, 1918): 657.

9. Quotation from Lawrence Veiller, "Industrial Housing Developments in America. I. Beloit, Wis. Eclipse Park," *Architectural Record* 43 (March 1918): 256.

10. Information from a survey of the "Eclipse Park Historical Area" prepared in 1981, collection of the Beloit Historical Society.

11. Craddock is outside Portsmouth. The firm also designed two smaller projects, which are not named; see "Honor Memory of Late Local Man, One Hundreth Anniversary of the Birth of George B. Post, Architect," *Bernardsville News,* January 20, 1938, clippings file, Bernardsville Public Library. See also "Post, James Otis," 108; and Leland M. Roth, *A Concise History of American Architecture* (New York: Harper & Row, 1979), 228–30.

INDEX

Numbers in **bold** refer to color-plate numbers;
numbers in *italics* refer to figure numbers.